The **Interviewing** Guidebook

The **Interviewing**
Guidebook

Joseph A. DeVito
Hunter College of the
City University of New York

Boston   New York   San Francisco
Mexico City   Montreal   Toronto   London   Madrid   Munich   Paris
Hong Kong   Singapore   Tokyo   Cape Town   Sydney

Contents

Welcome to *The Interviewing Guidebook* vii

The Nature of Interviewing 1
  The Interview Process 4
    Opening 4
    Feedforward 6
    Question-and-Answer Session 6
    Feedback 6
    Closing 7
  General Interview Structures 7
  Types of Interview Questions 9
    Neutral–Leading Questions 10
    Open–Closed Questions 11
    Primary–Follow-Up Questions 12
    Direct–Indirect Questions 12
  Ethical Considerations in Interviewing 13

The Information Interview 14
  Select the Person 15
  Secure an Appointment 16
  Prepare Your Questions 17
  Establish Rapport 17
  Tape the Interview 18
  Ask Open-Ended Questions 18
  Close and Follow Up the Interview 19

  Information Interview Preparation Guide 21

The Employment Interview 28
  Prepare Yourself 29
    Network 29
    Homework 34
  Prepare Your Résumé 38
    Types of Résumés 38
    Suggestions for Writing Your Résumé 45
    The Résumé Cover Letter 46
  Prepare Answers and Questions 47

Make an Effective Presentation of Self   49
Dress for Interview Success   53
Arrive on Time   54
Demonstrate Effective Interpersonal Communication   54
Acknowledge Cultural Rules and Customs   57
Mentally Review the Interview   61
Follow Up   61
The Lawfulness of Questions   68
 Recognizing Unlawful Questions   69
 Dealing with Unlawful Questions   71

Employment Interview Preparation Guide   74

Continuing Your Study of Interviewing   82

Summary of Concepts and Skills   83

Interviewing Exercises
Practicing Interviewing Skills   27
Preparing Your Résumé   46
Writing the Follow-Up Letter   68
Responding to Unlawful Questions   73

Interview for Analysis: Displaying Communication
Confidence in the Employment Interview   58

Glossary   87
Bibliography   91
Appendix: Additional Online Help   95
Index   99

Welcome to
The **Interviewing**
Guidebook

I nterviewing is one of the most important communication skills you can learn. It's crucial to getting the job you want, and ultimately the career you're preparing for right now. But such skills are not limited to the job interview; interviewing skills will also help you secure information and achieve a wide variety of communication goals identified throughout this discussion.

The Interviewing Guidebook focuses on two major types of interviews: the information-gathering interview, and the employment interview (along with the job résumé and the letters that are an essential part of the interview process). Other types of interviews are mentioned in passing (and guides to further exploration of these types are given) but they are not discussed in detail here.

The discussions of the informative and job interviews emphasize the skills you'll need to be successful in your own interviewing. Along with the text, which identifies the major interviewing skills and provides lots of examples to illustrate what works and what doesn't work, are a variety of features that should further help you master the skills of interviewing:

- **Interview Preparation Guides** provide worksheets for preparing both the information-gathering and the employment interviews. These will help you clarify your thoughts about the interview and will help you identify the major questions you need to consider for each type of interview.

- **Interviewing Exercises** are included to help you work actively with the concepts discussed here.

- **Interview for Analysis** is a transcript of a hypothetical interview that will enable you to see in concrete form effective and ineffective interviewing communication.

- **Online Help** notes identify websites that you should find useful.

- **What Would You Do?** scenarios will help you apply your interviewing skills to different situations.

- **Quotations** sprinkled throughout are designed to serve as "pause points," places in your reading where you'll find it useful to stop reading and ponder the implications of the quotation for your own interviewing experiences.

Unless I miss my guess, you're going to find interviewing an exciting and eminently practical communication skill. Good luck.

Joseph A. DeVito
jadevito@earthlink.net
http://tcbdevito.blogspot.com

The **Interviewing**
Guidebook

You'll no doubt find yourself in a wide variety of interview situations throughout your social and professional life. And, as you'll see throughout this brief book, your effectiveness in this form of communication will prove crucial in helping you achieve many of your life goals. This discussion covers three main topics: (1) the nature of interviewing, its characteristics, the nature of questions and answers, and the general types of interviews; (2) the information-gathering interview and the strategies to follow for greatest effectiveness; and (3) the employment interview and how you can best present yourself in this interview and in your résumé and cover letter.

The Nature of Interviewing

Interviewing is a particular form of communication in which you interact largely through a question-and-answer format to achieve a variety of specific goals or functions. Here are just a few such instances:

- A salesperson tries to persuade a client to buy a new car.
- A teacher talks with a student about the reasons the student failed the course.
- A grandchild talks with grandparents in an effort to record family history.
- A counselor talks with a family about their communication problems.

Interviewing Techniques

<u>Interview</u> I <u>Before</u> I <u>During</u> I <u>Questions</u> I <u>After</u>

A personal interview not only gives your potential employer an opportunity to evaluate you in depth and you a chance to sell yourself, but it also gives you the opportunity to learn much more about the employer and the company. It is important to be able to demonstrate your abilities to the interviewer and to show that you are an asset. By taking a few simple preparations, you can make a more favorable impression and minimize any nervousness you may feel during an interview.

Before the Interview

- Research Yourself
- Research the Company
- Practice the Interview

During the Interview

Interview Questions

- Questions Interviewers Ask
- Questions to Ask the Interviewer

After the Interview

Student Employment HOME I Learn I Benefit I Market I Apply I Site Map I Help

---

U.S. Department of the Interior
U.S. Geological Survey, 601 National Center, Reston, VA 20192, USA
URL http://www.usgs.gov/ohr/student/market/interview/index.html
Contact Sarah Griffin: students@usgs.gov
Last modification: 07-Oct-2004 (geb)

Figure 1
USGS Website (www.usgs.gov/ohr/student/market/interview/)
This is one example of a government website that contains useful information on interviewing.

- A recent graduate applies to Cisco for a job in the product development division.

- A doctor interviews a patient about past illnesses.

- A journalist interviews a political candidate.

- A Senate committee interviews the FCC chair.

- A building owner talks with a potential apartment renter.

- A minister talks with a church member about a membership drive.

- A lawyer examines a witness during a trial.

- A department's personnel committee interviews an application for a teaching position.

- A theatrical agent talks with a producer.

- A client discusses the qualities desired in a potential mate with a dating service employee.

- An employer talks with an employee about the reasons for terminating employment.

As you can see interviews serve a wide variety of functions—to persuade you to buy or sell, to inform you or to gain information from you, to counsel and support, and to uncover the truth, for example.

Most interviews follow a two-person structure, but team interviews are becoming increasingly popular. In the media—on "Nightline," for example—several journalists might interview a political candidate or one journalist might interview several candidates. On the ubiquitous television talk show, Oprah Winfrey, Jerry Springer, or Montel Williams will often interview several people at the same time. And anxious parents

> *In the hands of a skilled practitioner [the interview] is like a sharp knife that can cut away all the fat of irrelevant detail to get to the meat of the subject.*
>
> —JACK GRATUS

(and, in some cases, even members of the extended family) might interview their teenager's first dating partner.

In employment situations, team interviews are extremely important, especially as you go up the organizational hierarchy. It's common, for example, for an academic department or committee to interview a candidate for a teaching position, often followed by a similar team interview with the administration. In business organizations, three or four vice presidents might interview a candidate for a middle-management position.

The main advantage of the team interview is that it gives the audience or the organization different viewpoints and perspectives on the person being interviewed. It also helps ensure that the interview does not lag but follows a relatively rapid pace—especially important when the interview is on the Internet or on television.

Team interviews, however, are expensive and may degenerate into what may appear to be interrogations, a quality that may be desirable on television but inappropriate in an employment setting (see Kanter, 1995).

The Interview Process

In much the same way that you look at perception, listening, conversation, or interpersonal relationships, you can also view interviewing as a series of stages: opening, feedforward, question-and-answer format, feedback, closing, and follow-up (see Figure 2).

During all interviews, be especially alert for transitional cues that signal a move from one stage of the interview to the next. Don't continue to dwell on preliminaries after the interviewer has signaled a readiness to move to the next stage, for instance. As an interviewer, give cues that are easily understandable, and as an interviewee, watch carefully for and respond appropriately to these cues.

Opening   At the first stage interviewee and interviewer meet; the interview opens at that moment. Although this is an introductory stage and may seem to involve a "mere" exchange of common

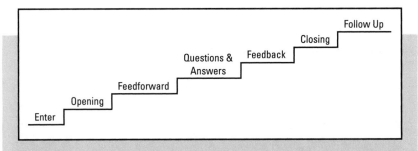

Figure 2
The Stages of the Interview

This model is designed to highlight the *general* process of interviewing, but it needs to be modified on the basis of the specific interview in which you may find yourself. View the stages as general categories that illustrate the natural progression of most interviews.

courtesies such as *hellos* and an exchange of names, an invitation to sit down, and perhaps a comment or two on the weather, this is a crucial part of the interview and you'll want to be at your best here as well as during the main phase of the interview. The conversation taking place at this stage is clearly preliminary and is more designed to make the situation comfortable than to communicate job-related information, say.

Feedforward   After this brief introductory exchange, the conversation narrows and focuses on the purpose of the interview. It provides a kind of feedforward as to what is going to happen next (for example, "I want to go over a few things on your résumé and then ask you a few questions about your training and so on"). You'll notice on the late-night talk shows that there is usually some preliminary communication and then the host focuses the interview on the real purpose the celebrity is there: "So I see you have a new movie out."

Question-and-Answer Session   Once the interview is focused, the question-and-answer session, the essential part of the interview, begins. If this is an information-gathering interview, then the questions will seek information and the interviewee will provide it, it is hoped. If this is an employment interview, the interviewer will attempt to discover your strengths and your weaknesses to get an impression of how suitable you'd be for the position, while you will attempt to present yourself as most suitable. At the same time, you may want to ask questions about the position, benefits, and so on. It is to this stage that most of the suggestions made throughout this book are addressed.

Feedback   After the questions are asked and the answers given, the interviewer will provide some basic feedback. Usually the feedback comes in the form of some positive comments and perhaps a summary of some significant part of the interview: "It was a pleasure meeting you. You sure seem like a person who thinks thoroughly before making decisions."

Closing   The closing is generally mixed in with the feedback and might go something like this: "Thanks for coming in to see us. I'm going to review your file and then I have a few more people to interview. So we'll be in touch with you within the next few weeks."

In all interviews, be especially alert to leave-taking cues. It's important that you recognize when the interviewer is saying the interview is over. Generally, it's best not to try to prolong the interview after clear leave-taking cues are given.

General Interview Structures

Interviews vary from relatively informal talks that resemble everyday conversations to those in which rigidly prescribed questions are asked in a set order (Hambrick, 1991). Depending on your specific purpose, you can select the interview structure, or combine various types to create a unique interview structure, that best fits your needs.

In the *informal interview* two friends might discuss what happened on their respective dates or employment interviews: *So tell me what happened? . . . And then what? . . . So what did you say? . . .* This type of interview resembles conversation; a general theme for the interview is chosen in advance but the specific questions are formed during the interaction. You use this type of interview to obtain information informally, as when you question another student regarding what happened in a class you missed. These interviews are highly nondirective—one person does not direct the other; rather each person responds much as she or he wants.

In the *guided interview*, a guest on "The Tonight Show" might be interviewed about a new CD or you might be interviewed for a job: *I see you have a new movie out. It looks like it's going to be a big hit. You play a senator. . . . Yeah, I play a senator from Hawaii who comes to Washington for the first time. And then the fun starts. . . .*

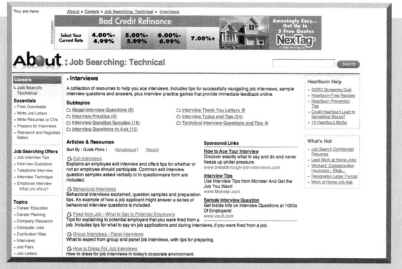

Figure 3

About Website (http://jobsearchtech.about.com/od/interview/)
As you can see this website contains lots of useful information on interviewing. About.com has lots of other useful, well-written, and easily accessed information on all aspects of professional career development.

Here the topics are chosen in advance but specific questions and wording are guided by the ongoing interaction. The guided interview is useful here because it ensures maximum flexibility in and responsiveness to the dynamics of the situation, though it is somewhat more directive than the informal interview.

The *standard open interview* might be used for interviewing several candidates for a job; you may want to ask each of them the exact same question so you can compare their responses: *We're taking on a new client, a paint company that wants to compete with the major manufacturers, so we'll need a total advertising plan in three months. Any ideas?* Open-ended questions and their order are selected in advance. This type of interview would be useful when standardization is needed, when you want to be sure to ask each person the same question in exactly the same way. This interview is highly directive; the interviewer guides the interview closely.

In the *quantitative interview* a researcher might survey students' political opinions. In this form, questions and their order are selected in advance as are the possible response categories, for example, A, B, C, D; agree–disagree; check from 1 to 10: *How often do you go to the dentist? (a) less than once a year, (b) once a year, (c) once every six months, (d) more often than every six months.* The quantitative interview is useful when statistical analyses are to be performed and when large amounts of information are to be collected. This is the most directive of all interviews; there is usually little opportunity to comment outside the rigidly prescribed format. Many of the popular books on relationships, sexual behavior, and child rearing, for example, are based on surveys that enable researchers to draw conclusions as to the age at which boys and girls start dating, the frequency of sexual behavior, and the most common child-rearing practices.

Types of Interview Questions

As already stated, the uniqueness of the interview is that it takes place in question-and-answer format. Consequently, understanding the different types of questions may help you ask questions more effectively (in an information-gathering interview) and respond to questions more effectively (in an employment interview). Questions may be analyzed in terms of at least the following dimensions: neutral–leading, open–closed, primary–follow-up, and direct–indirect.

As you read this section, recognize that asking questions is not the only way to elicit information from an interviewee. For example, after a question has been asked, you might paraphrase it (if you want the interviewee to expand on what she or he just said) or you might use minimal responses ("I see," "right") that encourage the interviewee to elaborate. And of course as an interviewer, you can always ask for more information ("That sounds interesting; tell me more").

Neutral–Leading Questions   Neutral questions and their opposite, leading questions, refer to the extent to which the question provides the answer the interviewer wants from the interviewee. Some questions are neutral and don't specify any answer as more appropriate than any other. At the other extreme are questions that are leading, or loaded. These clearly indicate the answer the interviewer expects or wants. Compare the following questions:

- How did you feel about managing your own web design firm?

- You must really enjoy managing your own web design company, don't you?

The first question is neutral and allows you to respond in any way; it asks for no particular answer. The second question is biased; it specifies that the interviewer expects a "yes." Between the neutrality of "How did you feel about your previous job?" and the bias of "You must have loved your previous job, didn't you?" there are questions that specify with varying degrees of strength the answer the interviewer expects or prefers. For example:

- Did you like your previous job?

- Did you dislike your previous job very much?

- It seems like it would be an interesting job, no?

An interviewer who asks too many biased questions will not learn about the interviewee's talents or experiences, but only about the interviewee's ability to give the desired answer. As an interviewee, pay special attention to any biases in the question. Don't give the responses your interviewer expects if they're not what you believe to be correct or know to be true. This would be unethical. However, when your responses are not what the interviewer expects, consider explaining why you're responding as you are. For example, to the biased question, "It seems like it would be an interesting job, no?" you might respond: "It was interesting most of the time, but I'm looking for a position that allows for greater creativity."

> *Occasionally, it [a biased or leading question] is used to test whether the interviewee has the courage to disagree, and how the interviewee handles pressure.*
> —SAM DEEP AND LYLE SUSSMAN

Open–Closed Questions Openness refers to the degree of freedom you have to respond, both in content and format. At times there's almost unlimited latitude in what may constitute an answer, for example, "What do you like to do most of all?" or "Why do you want to work at Peabody and Peabody?" At the opposite extreme are closed questions that require only a "yes" or "no," for example, "Are you willing to relocate to San Francisco?" and "Can you work with electronic spreadsheets?" Between these extremes are short-answer questions, those that are relatively closed and to which you have only limited freedom in responding, for example, "What would you do as manager here?" or "What computer skills do you have?" Part of the art of successful interviewing is to respond with answers that are appropriate to the question's level of openness. Thus if you're asked a question like "Why do you want to work at Peabody and Peabody?"

you're expected to speak at some length. If you're asked, "Are you willing to relocate to San Francisco?" then a simple "yes" or "no" (with or without a qualification) will suffice, for example, "Absolutely, though it would take me about six weeks to close my affairs here in Boston."

Primary–Follow-Up Questions Primary questions introduce a topic and are often relatively general ("What did you study in college?"). Follow-up questions ask for elaboration on what was just said ("I majored in economics too. What did you hate most about studying economics?"). Too many primary questions and not enough follow-up questions will often communicate a lack of interest and perhaps a failure to listen as effectively as possible. For example, if you're interviewing a scientist and ask only primary questions, it will easily appear as though you're just following a script and are not really prepared for the interview. Follow-up questions that ask for clarification, elaboration, or illustrations are essential to getting worthwhile information. A balance between primary and follow-up questions, determined in large part by the situation and by your own communication goals, should be your desired goal.

Direct–Indirect Questions Questions of these types will vary greatly from one culture to another. In the United States, be prepared for rather direct questions, whether you're being interviewed for information or for a job. In Japan, on the other hand, the interviewee is expected to reveal herself or himself despite the indirectness of the questions.

Similarly, cultures vary in what they consider appropriate directness in speaking of one's accomplishments, say, in a job interview. In many Asian cultures, the interviewee is expected to appear modest and unassuming and should allow his or her competences to emerge indirectly during the interview. In the United States, on the other hand, you're expected to state your competences without excessive modesty. In fact, many interviewers expect a certain amount of hyperbole and exaggeration.

Ethical Considerations in Interviewing

As you would in any form of communication, you incur ethical responsibilities in interviewing, particularly to respond honestly. At the same time, however, you want to present the best possible self you can and it's not always clear when legitimate self-praise slips into lying. Here are a few questions about which you'd have to make a decision between ethical and unethical self-presentation before responding.

Consider each of these questions that others might ask of you as asking for information that you have. For each question there are extenuating circumstances that make your responding fully or truthfully extremely difficult and that you are considering as you think of what to say (these are noted under "Thought").

Question: [An interviewer asks] You seem a bit old for this type of job. How old are you?

Thought: I am old for this job but I need it anyway. I don't want to turn the interviewer off by saying this is an illegal question because I really need this job, but I don't want to reveal my age either.

Question: [A friend asks your opinion] How do I look?

Thought: You look terrible, but I don't want to hurt your feelings.

Question: [A 15-year-old asks] Was I adopted? Who are my real parents?

Thought: Yes, you were adopted but I fear that you will look for your biological parents and will be hurt when you find that they are convicted felons.

Question: [A relationship partner of 20 years asks] Have you had any affairs since we've been together?

Thought: Yes, but I don't want to say anything because the affairs were insignificant (none are ongoing) and will only create problems for the one important relationship in my life.

Question: [A potential romantic partner asks] What's your HIV status?

Thought: I've never been tested, but now is not the time to talk about this. I'll practice safe sex so as not to endanger my partner.

Each reader will likely answer these questions differently, and each will develop her or his own ethics of interviewing. So as you read the remainder of this brief book, think about the ethics involved in both the information-gathering and the employment interviews.

The Information Interview

In the **information interview,** the interviewer tries to learn something about the interviewee. Variations on the basic informative interview would include, for example (Powell & Amsbary, 2006):

- journalistic interviews in which a journalist interviews newsmakers and then communicates this back to a large audience

- medical interviews in which a health professional seeks to learn a person's medical history

- oral history interviews of people who have witnessed important events as a way of writing history from the per-

---

▼ ONLINE HELP

Take a look at the Journalist's Toolbox (www.americanpressinstitute.org/content/4056.cfm). It contains a wealth of materials of use to the informative interviewer.

spective of those who lived it; younger family members increasingly are interviewing older members as a way of recording the history of their family

- police interrogations in which law enforcement personnel question witnesses or supposed law breakers in an effort to find out what really happened

In the information interview—unlike the employment interview—the person interviewed is usually an individual of some reputation and accomplishment. The interviewer accomplishes this goal by asking a series of questions designed to elicit the interviewee's views, beliefs, insights, perspectives, predictions, life history, and so on. Examples of the information interview include those published in popular magazines; TV interviews conducted by David Letterman, Katie Couric, and Barbara Walters; and those a lawyer conducts during a trial. All aim to elicit specific information from someone who supposedly knows something others don't know. Some of these interviews are informative on the surface but persuasive in main intent. For example, when a singer, writer, or actor comes on a talk show it is usually to sell something—a CD, a book, a recent film or television series.

In this discussion, we concentrate on your role as the interviewer, because that is the role in which you're likely to find yourself serving now and in the near future. Let's say that your interview is designed to get information about a particular field, for example, web design. You want to know about the available job opportunities and the preparation you would need to get into this field. Here are a few guidelines for conducting such information-gathering interviews.

Select the Person

There are several ways to find a likely person to interview. Let's say that you wish to learn something about web publishing. You might, for example, look through your college catalog; there you find that a course on this general topic is offered by Professor Bernard Brommel. You think it might be worthwhile to interview him. Or you visit a variety of newsgroups and discover that one particular person has posted extremely well-reasoned articles and you'd like to interview her to get her opinion on web design and advice on how you might break into this field. If you want to contact a book author, you can always write to the author in care of the publisher or editor (listed on the copyright page), although many authors are now including their e-mail address. You can often find the address and phone number of most professional people by calling the appropriate professional association for a directory listing (the *Encyclopedia of Associations* lists nearly every professional association in the country). Or you can write to the person via the association's website. Newsgroup and listserv writers are the easiest to contact because their e-mail addresses are included with their posts.

> *To question a wise person is the beginning of wisdom.*
> —GERMAN PROVERB

After you've selected one of the people you hope to interview but before you pursue the interview, try to learn something about this person. Consult an online library or bookstore to see if this person has written a book, or go through a CD-ROM database to see if this person has written any research articles. Search through the databases covering computers, the Internet, and the World Wide Web. Search the Web and Usenet groups to see if the person has a web page or posts to newsgroups. You may find that the person encourages people to correspond via e-mail.

Secure an Appointment

Phone the person or send a letter or e-mail requesting an interview. In your call or letter, identify the purpose of your request and that

---

▼ **ONLINE HELP**

You can often find experts through a variety of websites, for example, www.experts.com and http://www.usc.edu/dept/news_service/experts_directory.html.

you would like a brief interview. For example, you might say: "I'm preparing for a career in web design and I would appreciate it if I could interview you to learn more about the subject. The interview would take about 15 minutes." (It's helpful to let the person know it will not take too long; she or he is more likely to agree to being interviewed.) Generally, it's best to be available at the interviewee's convenience. So indicate flexibility on your part, for example, "I can interview you any afternoon this week."

You may find it necessary to conduct the interview by phone. In this case, call to set up a time for a future interview call. For example, you might say, "I'm interested in a career in web design and I would like to interview you on the job opportunities in this field. If you agree, I can call you back at a time that's convenient for you." In this way, you don't run the risk of asking the person to participate in an interview while eating lunch, talking with colleagues, or running to class.

Prepare Your Questions

Preparing questions ahead of time will ensure that you use the time available to your best advantage. Of course, as the interview progresses other questions will come to mind and should be asked. But having a prepared list of questions will help you obtain the information you need most easily. Do be careful, however, that you don't read your questions. Much as you would lose spontaneity if you read a public speech, you lose spontaneity if you read your questions. So perhaps after writing your list of questions, you might want to create a reminder list consisting of only a few words and phrases. If you practice with this list, you'll be likely to cover all the important questions you want to ask and at the same time communicate in a conversational style.

Establish Rapport

Open the interview with an expression of thanks for making the time available to you. Many people receive lots of requests and it helps if

> **? WHAT DO YOU SAY?**
> You finally got the opportunity to interview on the campus radio station a famous author who is notorious for being difficult. You need to establish rapport right at the start of the interview. *What do you say?*

you also remind the person of your specific purpose. You might say something like: "I really appreciate your making time for this interview. As I mentioned, I'm preparing a speech on the job opportunities in web design and your expertise and experience in this area will help a great deal."

After you've established rapport, you ask your first question. On the basis of the answers to your first few questions—their length and tone—you'll be able to judge the kinds of questions that will work best and how you can use follow-up questions to get more detail.

Tape the Interview

Generally, it's a good idea to tape the interview. It will enable you to secure a more complete record of the interview, which you'll be able to review as you need to. It will also free you to concentrate on the interview rather than on trying to write down the person's responses. But ask permission first. Some people prefer not to have informal interviews taped. Even if the interview is being conducted by phone, ask permission if you intend to tape the conversation.

> **? WHAT DO YOU SAY?**
> You're interviewing an 80-year-old writer about romantic affairs with famous movie stars. But instead of being forthright, as you anticipated, your interviewee expresses an embarrassment to speak of such things with such a young interviewer as you. This part of the writer's life is crucial to the magazine for which you're writing the interview. *What do you say?*

Ask Open-Ended Questions

Use questions that provide the person you're interviewing with room to discuss the issues you want to raise. Thus, instead of asking "Do you have formal training in web publishing?" (a question that requires a simple "yes" or "no" and will not be very informative), you might ask, "Can you tell me something about your background in this field?" (an open-ended question that allows the person greater freedom in responding). You can then ask follow-up questions to pursue more specifically the topics raised in the answers to your open-ended questions.

Close and Follow Up the Interview

At the end of the interview, thank the person for making the time available for the interview, for being informative, cooperative, helpful, or whatever. Showing your appreciation will make it a lot easier if you want to return for a second interview. Within the next two or three days, follow up the interview with a brief note of thanks that expresses your appreciation for the time given you, your enjoyment in speaking with the person, and your pleasure in accomplishing your goal of getting the information you needed. Figure 4 on page 20 shows a sample letter.

123 Walnut Street (Apt. 3C)
New York, New York 10038-1525
May 30, 2008

Ms. Anita Brice
Brice Publishers, Inc.
17 Michigan Avenue (Suite 233)
Chicago, Illinois 60600-2345

Dear Ms. Brice:

It was a pleasure meeting you on Tuesday. Thanks for taking the time to talk to me. I greatly appreciate your sharing your knowledge of the desktop publishing industry as well as your insights into the future of this business.

I now have a much more complete understanding of the field. Understanding your background and experience has also given me a clear idea of the kinds of skills I'll need to succeed in this growing industry.

Again, thank you for your time and your willingness to share your expertise. I wish you continued success.

Sincerely,

Carlos Villas

Carlos Villas

Figure 4
A Sample Letter of Thanks for an Information Interview

INFORMATION INTERVIEW PREPARATION GUIDE

Here are a few questions that will help you plan for the information interview. The questions are designed to help you focus the interview and to anticipate any possible problem areas. This added preparation will also help to reduce any apprehension and give you more of a sense of control over the interview process.

1. **Opening.** How will you open the interview? List one, two, or three things you might say in opening the interview that go beyond the simple "Thank you for agreeing to be interviewed." Next, identify what purpose you hope to accomplish with each opening statement.

Opening Statement	Opening Statement Purpose
1. _____	1. _____
_____	_____
_____	_____
_____	_____
_____	_____
_____	_____
2. _____	2. _____
_____	_____
_____	_____
_____	_____
_____	_____
_____	_____
3. _____	3. _____
_____	_____
_____	_____
_____	_____
_____	_____
_____	_____

2. **Goals.** List two or three goals you want to accomplish in the interview and what strategies you'd use to accomplish these goals.

General Interview Goals

Strategies for Accomplishing Your Goals

1. _____

1. _____

2. _____

2. _____

3. _____

3. _____

3. **Questions.** What questions do you want to ask? List five major questions that you want to ask. For each question, consider the interviewee's anticipated response, and identify at least one possible follow-up question.

Major Questions	Follow-Up Questions
1. _____	1. _____
_____	_____
_____	_____
_____	_____
_____	_____
_____	_____
_____	_____
_____	_____
_____	_____
2. _____	2. _____
_____	_____
_____	_____
_____	_____
_____	_____
_____	_____
_____	_____
_____	_____
3. _____	3. _____
_____	_____
_____	_____
_____	_____
_____	_____
_____	_____
_____	_____
_____	_____

4. **Closing.** How will you close the interview? List two or three goals you want to accomplish in closing the interview and what specifically you'll say to accomplish these goals.

Closing Goals	Communicating the Goals
1. _____	1. _____
2. _____	2. _____
3. _____	3. _____

5. **Problems.** What possible problems might arise as you conduct this information interview? List two or three possible problems and what you'd do if they did occur.

Possible Problems

Possible Ways to Handle the Problems

1. _____ 1. _____
   _____   _____
   _____   _____
   _____   _____
   _____   _____
   _____   _____
   _____   _____
   _____   _____

2. _____ 2. _____
   _____   _____
   _____   _____
   _____   _____
   _____   _____
   _____   _____
   _____   _____
   _____   _____

3. _____ 3. _____
   _____   _____
   _____   _____
   _____   _____
   _____   _____
   _____   _____
   _____   _____
   _____   _____

6. **Follow-Up.** How will you follow up the interview? Write a paragraph of what you'd say in a phone, e-mail, or letter follow-up.

Practicing Interviewing Skills

Form three-person groups, preferably among persons who don't know each other well or who have had relatively little interaction. One person should be designated the interviewer, another the interviewee, and the third the interview analyst. The interview analyst should choose one of the following situations:

1. An interview for the position of camp counselor for children with disabilities
2. An interview for a part in a new Broadway musical
3. A therapy interview to focus on communication problems in relating to superiors
4. A teacher–student interview in which the teacher is trying to discover why the course taught last semester was such a dismal failure
5. An interview between the chair of the communication department and a candidate for the position of instructor of human communication

After the situation is chosen, the interviewer should interview the interviewee for approximately 10 minutes. The analyst should observe but not interfere in any way. After the interview is over, the analyst should offer a detailed analysis, considering each of the following:

1. What happened during the interview (essentially a description of the interaction)?
2. What was handled well?
3. What went wrong? What aspects of the interview were not handled as effectively as they might have been?
4. What could have been done to make the interview more effective?

The analyst for each interview may then report the major findings to the whole class. The group leader may then develop a list of "common faults" or "suggestions for improving interviews."

The Employment Interview

Perhaps of most concern to college students is the **employment interview.** In this type of interview, a great deal of information and persuasion will be exchanged. The interviewer will learn about you, your interests, your talents—and, if clever enough, some of your weaknesses and liabilities. In turn, you'll be informed about the nature of the company, its benefits, its advantages—and, if you're clever enough, some of its disadvantages and problems. The interviewer may persuade you of the benefits of working for the company and you'll persuade the interviewer that you're the right person for the job.

Today, the employment interview is likely to be an important part of your professional life, beyond getting your initial job. You'll likely interview for jobs throughout your professional life. And even when you stay with the same company, you're likely to interview for promotions and different positions. In addition, you're likely to participate in at least two other kinds of workplace interviews once you do get the job:

- In the **appraisal interview,** management or more experienced colleagues assess the interviewee's performance. The general aim is to discover what the interviewee is doing well (and to praise this) and not doing well and why (and to sug-

---

▼ ONLINE HELP

Many colleges and universities maintain open websites devoted to employment interviewing. For example, the career center of the School of Business at the University of Wisconsin provides numerous aids for effective job interviewing, including a sample mock interview video (www.bus.wisc.edu/ career). The University of South Carolina at Spartanburg (www.uscs.edu/ student_life/career_center) and the University of Dayton (http://careers/ udayton.edu) also have excellent and practical websites to help prepare you further for that important job interview.

gest correctives). These interviews are important because they help new members of an organization see how their performance matches up with the expectations of those making promotion and firing decisions. They make clear what you'll need to do to advance in the organization and perhaps how you might go about it.

■ In the **exit interview,** used widely by organizations in the United States and throughout the world, management tries to discover why an employee is leaving the company. Because all organizations compete in one way or another for superior workers, when an employee leaves a company voluntarily, it's important to know why, to prevent other valuable workers from leaving as well. When the employee is not leaving voluntarily, this exit interview functions to provide a way of making the exit as pleasant and as efficient as possible for both employee and employer.

Prepare Yourself

Before going into a job interview, prepare yourself. One way to do this is through general long-term preparation, especially networking, and the second way is to do your homework for the specific interview.

Network   Networking is especially important in finding a job and, in the popular mind, is often viewed as having this one major function. Actually networking is a much broader process that can be viewed as one of using other people's suggestions and experiences to help you solve your problems or at least offer insights that bear on your problem—for example, how to publish your manuscript, where to look for low-cost auto insurance, how to find an affordable apartment, or how to empty your cache.

Networking has at least two forms: informal and formal. Informal networking is what we do every day when we find ourselves in a

ℐℐ CAREER SERVICES

SOUTHEAST

University Center 008 - 4201 Grant Line Road ~ New Albany, IN 47150
PHONE: (812) 941-2275 FAX: (812) 941-2557

QUICK LINKS

Students
Register / Login to my account
Employers
Register / Login to my account

JOBS

- Job Fair Information
- Search Job Listings
- Post Your Resume
- Work Study Information
- Volunteer Opportunities
- Other Internet Job Sites

CAREER TOOLS

- Choosing a Major
- Exploring Careers
- Discovering Career Interests
- More Career Tools . . .

INTERNSHIPS

- Student Information
- Employer Information
- Faculty Information
- Internship Forms

RESUME TIPS

- Resume Writing Tips
- Job Correspondence

INTERVIEWING TIPS

- Interview Techniques
- Dress for Success
- Telephone Tips
- Research Employers
- Market Yourself
- Relocation Services

TIPS

Interviewing Techniques and Tips

Typical Interview Styles and Questions - Employers often use a behavioral or traditional style of interviewing.

Questions for You to Ask the Employer - Employers expect candidates to have meaningful questions to ask at the interview.

15 Ways to Blow an Interview - What NOT to do in the interview.

Recruiter Evaluation Criteria - How are you rated and evaluated?

Informational Interviewing - A different type of interview. This is good.

Interviewing is both art and science. To be most successful, understand the process, prepare for known situations, and anticipate the next move.

The purpose of an interview between a candidate and a prospective employer is to exchange information. Candidates have particular qualifications, skills and strengths to offer and prospective employers want to purchase certain qualifications, skills and strengths that will fill their needs. Candidates and employers must be certain that the match is correct.

There are four phases to a typical interview:

1. **Introduction.** During this first phase of the interview, both the candidate and employer are establishing first impressions, making personal introductions, and establishing rapport.

2. **Background and Probe Stage.** The prospective employer will ask the candidate about educational background and work experience. The employer will discuss skills and abilities in more detail, relative to the employer's needs. This is the questioning period.

Figure 5

Indiana University Southeast Website (www.careerservices.ius.edu/tips/interviews/interviewprep.html)

College websites are probably the most useful when it comes to locating helpful material on interviewing. Most such websites are open to everyone and can be accessed easily through your favorite search engine.

Courtesy of Indiana University Southeast Career Services Office. Copyright © 2004 Indiana University Trustees.

new situation or unable to answer questions. Thus, for example, if you're new at a school, you might ask someone in your class where's the best place to eat or shop for new clothes or who's the best teacher for interpersonal communication. In the same way, when you enter a new work environment, you might ask more experienced workers how to perform certain tasks or who to avoid or approach when you have questions.

Formal networking is the same, except that it's a lot more systematic and strategic. It's the establishment of connections with people who can help you by answering questions, getting you a job, helping you get promoted, or helping you relocate or accomplish any task you want to accomplish.

At the most obvious level, you can network with people you already know. If you review the list of people in your acquaintance, you'll probably discover that you know a great number of people with very specialized knowledge who can be of assistance to you in a wide variety of ways. In some cultures, Brazil is one example, friendships are established in part because of the potential networking connections that a particular person has (Rector & Neiva, 1996). You can also network with people who know people you know. Thus you may contact a friend's friend to find out if the firm she or he works for is hiring. Or you may contact people you have no connection with. Perhaps you've read something the person wrote or you've heard the person's name raised in connection with an area you're interested in and you want to get more information. With e-mail addresses so readily available, it's now common to e-mail individuals who have particular expertise and ask them questions you might have.

▼ ONLINE HELP

Take the interviewing quiz "Are you ready for your next interview?" offered by UCLA's Career Center (http://career.UCLA.edu/jobsrch/interview/).

In college you have a variety of networking opportunities. In fact, one of the great values of college is that it provides a wide variety of opportunities for networking now and throughout your professional career. The clubs you belong to will often invite prominent speakers (who may well be influential in companies you may want to join). The internships that many academic departments are encouraging students to enter will often offer a wide variety of networking possibilities—from assistants who can tell you when openings will be available to management personnel who might offer advice, employment leads, and recommendations. Working in community-based programs—another initiative in many colleges—will likewise offer networking opportunities.

The great value of networking, of course, is that it provides you with access to a wealth of specialized information. At the same time, it often makes accessing that information a lot easier than if you had to find it by yourself.

In networking, it's often recommended that you try to establish relationships that are mutually beneficial. After all, much as others are useful sources of information for you, you're likely to be a useful source of information for others. And so if you can provide others with helpful information, it's more likely that they will provide helpful information to you. In this way, a mutually satisfying and productive network is established.

Some networking experts advise you to develop files and directories of potentially useful sources that you can contact for needed information. For example, if you're a freelance artist, you might develop a list of persons who might be in a position to offer you work or who might lead you to others who might offer such work. Authors, editors, art directors, administrative assistants, people in advertising, and a host of others might eventually provide useful leads for such work. Creating a directory of such people and keeping in contact with them on a fairly regular basis can often simplify your obtaining freelance work.

Formal networking requires that you take an active part in locating and establishing connections. Be proactive; initiate contacts

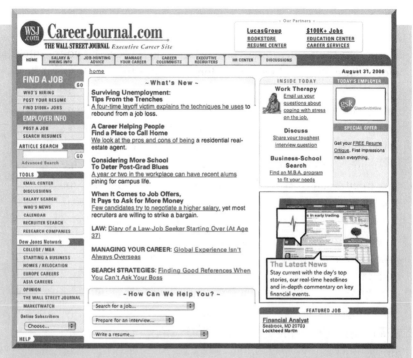

Figure 6

Career Journal (www.careerjournal.com)

CareerJournal.com, maintained by the *Wall Street Journal*, one of the premier financial newspapers, contains all sorts of professional and career advice. The material on interviewing is current, well-written, and extremely practical.

Reprinted with permission of Dow Jones & Company, Inc.

rather than wait for them to come to you. Of course, this can be overdone; you don't want to rely on people to do the work you can easily do yourself. And yet, if you're also willing to help others, there is nothing wrong in asking these same people to help you. If you're respectful of their time and expertise, it's likely that your networking attempts will be successful. Following up your requests with thank-you notes, for example, will help you establish networks that can be ongoing productive relationships rather than one-shot affairs.

> **? WHAT DO YOU SAY?**
> One of your colleagues has taken networking to its ugliest extreme and asks everyone for information without ever once trying to find it on his own. Today he comes to you for a phone number that he can easily find in his own directory. You're fed up. *What do you say?*

Homework   Interviewing experts suggest that doing your homework consists of researching four areas: the field, the position, the company, and current events (Taub, 1997).

First, research the career field you're entering and its current trends. With this information you'll be able to demonstrate that you're up-to-date and committed to the area you want this company to pay you to work in.

Second, research the specific position you're applying for so you'll be able to show how your skills and talents mesh with the position. A good way to do this is to visit the company's website and "job shadow," that is, follow a person who does essentially what you'd be hired to do. Many schools are now instituting job-shadowing

> **▼ ONLINE HELP**
> Read more about job shadowing. The Wake Country Public School System website explains job shadowing in education (www.wcpss.net/ school_to_career/work_based_learning/job_shadow/). Also see JobWeb.com, which contains information on job shadowing and other topics relevant to the job search.

Figure 7

Monster Board (www.monster.com)

Monster Board lists thousands of jobs you can access by keyword, location, or industry; it's just one of the many websites that are useful for finding jobs. Take a look at a few others; for example: www.flipdog.com identifies thousands of job opportunities and allows you to post your résumé; www.careerpath.com organizes the classified ads from leading newspapers; and www.jobtrak.com is especially valuable for college students looking for their first job or for internships.

Reprinted with permission of Monster.com.

programs to help their students become familiar with specific jobs. Your college's career center will likely have more information on job shadowing.

Also, most large corporations and, increasingly, many small firms, maintain websites and frequently include detailed job descriptions. Prepare yourself to demonstrate your ability to perform each of the tasks noted in the job description. Figure 7 on page 35 shows the home page of the Monster Board which will give you a good starting place in searching websites to learn about jobs and specific companies and even to improve your résumé.

Third, research the company or organization—its history, mission, and current directions. If it's a publishing company, familiarize yourself with their books and software products. If it's an advertising agency, familiarize yourself with their major clients and major advertising campaigns. A good way to do this is to call and ask the company to send you any company brochures, newsletters, or perhaps a quarterly or annual report. And be sure to visit their website; not only will it provide you with lots of useful information about this company but it also will show the interviewer that you make use of the latest technology. With extensive knowledge of the company, you'll be able to show your interest and focus on this specific company. One excellent way to do this is to set a news alert on your computer. For example, you can set an alert for the name of the company you're planning to interview with and you'll be sent links to news items in which the name of the company appears. Figure 8 is a web screen of Google Alerts, one of several services that allow you to set up these alerts. Of course, you can also use this free service to be alerted to items you're researching for your classes.

Fourth, research what is going on in the world in general and in the business world in particular. This will help you to demonstrate your breadth of knowledge and that you're a knowledgeable individual who continues to learn. Reading a good daily newspaper or a weekly news magazine should help you in mastering current events.

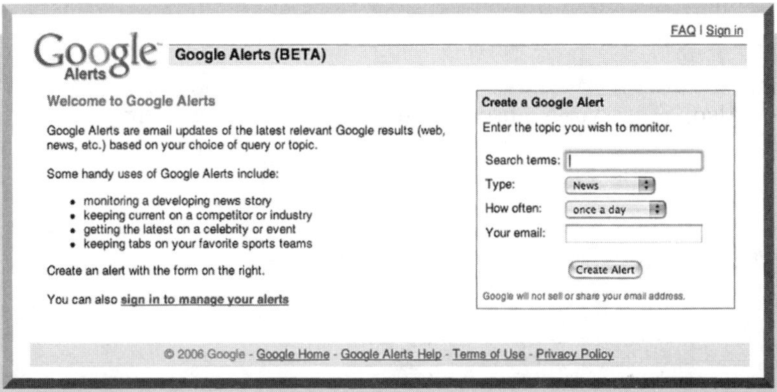

Screenshot content:

Google Alerts

Google Alerts (BETA)

Welcome to Google Alerts

Google Alerts are email updates of the latest relevant Google results (web, news, etc.) based on your choice of query or topic.

Some handy uses of Google Alerts include:

- monitoring a developing news story
- keeping current on a competitor or industry
- getting the latest on a celebrity or event
- keeping tabs on your favorite sports teams

Create an alert with the form on the right.

You can also sign in to manage your alerts

Create a Google Alert

Enter the topic you wish to monitor.

Search terms:

Type: News

How often: once a day

Your email:

(Create Alert)

Google will not sell or share your email address.

© 2006 Google - Google Home - Google Alerts Help - Terms of Use - Privacy Policy

Figure 8
Google Alerts

As you can see from this easy-to-navigate screen, you can customize your alerts in several ways with just a few mouse clicks. Also take a look at Yahoo's similar service at http://alerts.yahoo.com.
Screenshot © Google Inc. and is used with permission.

With the employment interview, both you and the company are trying to fill a need. You want a job that will help build your career, and the company wants an effective employee who will be an asset to the company. View the interview as an opportunity to engage in a joint effort to gain something beneficial. If you approach the interview in this cooperative frame of mind, you are much less likely to become defensive, which in turn will make you a more appealing potential colleague.

> *Most people who fail to get the job they really want fail not because they are not qualified but because they failed in the interview. And most failure occurs because they aren't prepared.*
>
> —David W. Crawley, Jr.

Prepare Your Résumé

The most important document you can prepare is your résumé. A résumé is a summary of essential information about your experience, education, and abilities. Often, a job applicant submits a résumé in response to a job listing, and if the employer thinks the applicant's résumé is promising, the candidate is invited for an interview. Figure 9 on page 40 is a sample résumé that highlights the types of information you need to include in your own résumé.

When you are preparing your résumé, consider the advantages of preparing a business card too. Word-processing programs make this easy and inexpensive and, of course, you can change the information with little effort. Try to follow one of the business card templates that come with your word processor or desktop publishing program. In this way you'll be sure to include the necessary information, omit the nonessential, and present it in a well-designed format.

Types of Résumés   Each occupation seems to prefer a somewhat different résumé, so before preparing your own résumé investigate the kind of résumés employees in your field prefer and tailor your history and competences to that specific kind of résumé. Amid this diversity, however, there are three main résumé types: chronological, functional, and curriculum vitae.

Figure out what your most magnificent qualities are and make them indispensable to the people you want to work with. Notice that I didn't say "work for."

—LINDA BLOODWORTH THOMASON

The Chronological Résumé. The chronological résumé organizes your experience (if possible, in terms of the job titles you've held) beginning with the most recent or current position and working back through your work history. This résumé provides just the right amount of information to be easily and quickly skimmed by the busy personnel manager.

A chronological résumé will work well for you if you have had a continuous history of jobs that can demonstrate your growth—from, say, entry-level positions to ones of greater and greater authority. If you don't have this experience, then this résumé may not work for you—right now. It may be the type of résumé you'll write five or ten years from now. A sample chronological résumé appears in Figure 10 on page 42.

The Functional Résumé. Whereas the chronological résumé organizes your experience in terms of time units, the function résumé organizes your experience in terms of your competences or skills. Employers like this type of résumé when they can easily identify the competences they are looking for in a new hire in your résumé. If you anticipate that they may not be able to match what they

---

▼ ONLINE HELP

The career website of the University of North Carolina at Chapel Hill has a detailed section on résumés, identifying the kinds of information you should include and showing sample chronological résumés (www.unc.edu/depts/ career). Cal State at San Bernardino also maintains an excellent website with sample chronological, functional, and combination résumés (http://career.csusb.edu).

(1) Ramona Morales
57-12 Horace Harding Expressway #15D
Corona, NY 11368
(718) 555-0005
r/morales@xyz.com

(2) Objective

To secure a position with a college textbook publisher in marketing and sales.

(3) Employment Experience

Bookstore Assistant, Queens College Bookstore
2006–present
- Maintained shelf stock
- Managed inventory database
- Placed orders with textbook publishers
- Assisted with front desk operations, including client interaction, operating cash register, typing, and filing

Front Desk Employee, Queens College Library
2005
- Responsible for periodical library
- Checked books in and out at front desk
- Acted as liaison for interlibrary loan books
- Offered general information about college library, the online catalog system, interlibrary loans, and the Internet terminals

Retail sales and management, luggage department, Macy's Department Store, Queens Center

(4) Education

Queens College, BA expected 2008

Major: Communication (Emphasis on interpersonal communication and public relations)
Minor: Marketing
12 Credits in Computer Science
LaGuardia Community College, AA, 2002
Major: Business

(5) Activities

- Vice President, Debate Club, Queens College, 2004–2005
- Member, Championship Debate Team, Eastern Division, 2005
- Literacy Volunteer for Spanish-speaking grade school students in English at PS 150, 2004
- Class Treasurer, LaGuardia Community College, 2001–2002
- Member, Young Business Person's Association

(6) Skills and Competencies

- Word processing
- Working knowledge of Microsoft Excel and Lotus 1-2-3
- Knowledge of HTML language inventory software
- Bilingual in English and Spanish, capable in French
- Excellent interpersonal and public speaking skills

(7) References

Available upon request.

(8)

Figure 9
A Sample Functional Résumé

1 Your name, address, phone and fax number, and e-mail are generally centered at the top ofthe résumé.

2 For some people, employment objectives may be more general than indicated here; for example, "to secure a management trainee position with an international investment bank." If you have more specific objectives, put them down. Don't imply that you'll take just anything, but don't appear too specific or demanding, either.

3 List work experience in chronological order, beginning with your latest position and working back. Depending on your work experience, you may have to pare down what you write. Or, if you have little or nothing to write, you may have to search through your employment history for some relevant experience. Often, the dates of the various positions are included. If you have little or no paid work experience or large gaps in employment history due, say, to time off raising a family, include volunteer work or other unpaid work that requires skills important to the job; for example, coordinator of a little league team or treasurer of the PTA.

4 Provide more information than simply your educational degree. For example, include your major and your minor and perhaps sequences of courses in communication or management or some other field that will further establish your suitability for the job. List honors or awards if they're relevant to your education or job experience. If the awards are primarily educational (for example, Dean's List), list them under the Education heading; if job-related, list them under the Employment Experience heading.

5 Identify those activities that are relevant to the job skills you want to demonstrate (for example, debating) and also those that attest to the personal qualities you want to stress (for example, reliability and trustworthiness, as shown in being treasurer).

6 Highlight your special skills. Do you have some foreign language ability? Do you have experience with business or statistical software? If you do, put it down. Such competencies are relevant to many jobs.

7 Some interview experts recommend you include on your résumé the names of references, people who can attest to your abilities and character. If you do this, include these names—each with address, phone numbers, and e-mail address— at the end of the résumé under a References heading. Usually, however, you mention in your cover letter that references are available upon request.

8 Make sure your résumé creates the impression you want to make. Typographical errors, incorrect spelling, poorly spaced headings and entries, and generally sloppy work will make a negative impression.

ROBIN A. JOBSEEKER

18013 Future Drive
Northridge, CA 91330

(818)555-2738
Willing to Travel/Relocate

OBJECTIVE	**Pharmaceutical Sales Representative**
EDUCATION	**B.A. Degree—Biology, January 20xx** California State University, Northridge

Science Courses with Laboratories:
- Medical Microbiology
- Medical Mycology
- Cellular Physiology
- Genetics

- Human Anatomy
- Cell Biology
- Human Physiology
- Chemistry

Business Courses:
- Marketing
- Business Law

HONORS   GPA: 3.2   Dean's List: 2 semesters

ACTIVITIES   Vice President, CSUN Biology Club
Sigma Alpha Epsilon Fraternity

RELEVANT
EXPERIENCE
3/xx
to
present

Customer Service Representative
BelAir Surgical Supply, Van Nuys, California
- Provide customers and 30+ outside sales personnel with product/ service information
- Open new accounts and coordinate customer relations
- Prepare sales statistics and graphs

11/xx
to
2/xx

Sales Associate
Sears, Roebuck and Company, Northridge, California
- Demonstrated and sold a variety of floor merchandise
- Provided customer service in high volume catalog sales department
- Supervised and trained two employees
- Opened new accounts and conducted credit checks
- Received "Employee of the Month" award

5/xx
to
9/xx

Manager/Trainer
Six Flags Magic Mountain, Valencia, California
- Managed three general merchandise stores
- Supervised and scheduled 40+ employees
- Trained employees to work in games and retail areas

ADDITIONAL
EXPERIENCE

Part-Time and Summer Employment:
Construction Worker, File Clerk, Food Service

Figure 10
A Sample Chronological Résumé
From California State University, Northridge, Career Center
www.csun.edu/career/sampleresumes/sampleresumes_chronol.

want with what you offer (let's say the job description was somewhat vague and it wasn't clear to you exactly what skills they were looking for), try to describe what you did and perhaps how you did it. This will help the employer see what you might do for them. For example, if you list "bookkeeping" as one of your skills, you might also describe your bookkeeping experience in a bit more detail by saying, for example:

- Maintained the income and expense accounts for a bookstore with sales in excess of $3 million and a staff of 20.
- Supervised college intern bookkeepers for three years.

Even when you use the functional résumé to emphasize your skills, also include a brief chronological history of your work experience to help the employer see the continuity among jobs and the progression of responsibilities. A sample functional résumé is presented in Figure 9 on page 40.

The Curriculum Vitae. The curriculum vitae (CV; sometimes called an academic vitae) is a different kind of résumé and would be used by, for example, your college professors when applying for teaching positions or a scientist applying for a job with a pharmaceutical company. The CV is a list of your accomplishments. For example, a college professor might organize her or his CV under such categories as Education (identifying the degrees earned and the institutions from which they were earned), Publications, Courses Taught, and Service (to professional associations, to the college, and to the community). Lots of curricula vitae (CVs) are online and you may find it interesting to locate CVs of professors at your college or professors who have conducted research you've read. You can look at my CV by going to the Communication Blog

---

▼ ONLINE HELP

The University of Alabama maintains a great website with interviewing advice and résumés for just about every field you can image (www.uacc.ua.edu/content).

(http://tcbdevito.blogspot.com) and clicking "vita." This CV is a bit more informal and selective (with asides about certain textbooks) than most academic CVs, as you'll see when you visit some of the other sites for CVs.

In addition to the suggestions offered here and on the various websites mentioned, a variety of computer programs are available to help you in preparing your résumé. Most offer an extensive array of templates that you fill in (or customize if you wish) with your specific data. The one presented in Figure 9 (page 40), for example, was customized from a Corel Office Suite template. Microsoft Word offers excellent templates; you can access the Résumé Wizard by going to File/New/New Document tab/New from Template/General Templates/Other Documents/Résumé Wizard (double click). There you'll find templates for professional, contemporary, and elegant styles and for entry-level, chronological, functional, and professional résumés.

Any résumé may be submitted in hard copy or in electronic form. The way you submit your résumé will be determined by the company to which you're applying. Often, though this is certainly changing, small organizations welcome hard copy résumés. Larger and especially multinational organizations may ask for electronic résumés that they can scan into a database and attempt to match their needs with the competences on the résumés. The "matchup" is done by searching for key words, so be sure to include the terms in your résumé that you believe this employer might be looking for.

Key words will naturally vary with the type of job in which you're interested. The best source for finding these key words is the job description for the position you want. Note especially the nouns in the description and try to use these (when appropriate) in your résumé. Another way to find the key words is to visit the website of the company you want to interview with as well as other companies in the same field; you'll quickly pick up the jargon of the field and some key words you can use. And, of course, if you have the opportunity, network with people in the field; listen to how they talk and seek their expertise on key words.

You can also post your résumé on the Internet through a variety of websites. For example, www.careermosaic.com will post your résumé for four months. At Monster.com (www.monster.com) you can post your résumé and the type of job you're looking for, and you will receive e-mail when an appropriate job is posted.

Suggestions for Writing Your Résumé Together with the previous discussion on the types of résumés, the sample résumés, and the suggestions offered on the numerous websites, the following suggestions will help you write an effective and successful résumé.

- Gain attention. Interviewers and recruiters spend only a few seconds looking

  Everybody looks good on paper.
  —JOHN Y. BROWN

  through the pile of résumés that reach their desks. So make your résumé jump out—not with garish color or graphics but with excellence in style and format.

- Proofread, proofread, proofread. Check spelling, grammar, and punctuation as though your job depended on it, because it does.

- Use the same quality paper, laser printer, and clear and easily readable font that doesn't look like the old-fashioned typing (as courier does) for both your résumé and your cover letter (discussed below). Laser-printed résumés scan a lot better than those written with dot matrix or bubble jet printers.

- Tell the truth. Don't make up experience, pad your GPA, or exaggerate your competences.

- Test drive your résumé. Before sending out your résumé, have others look it over and get some feedback. College career centers often offer this service; if not, then try passing it by a helpful professor or a more experienced friend.

- Include key words in your résumé. Because many résumés are scanned into huge databases and searched on the basis of key words, use the words that a recruiter would use in looking for someone to fulfill the job you want.

- Use powerful words. In writing your résumé, use verbs that communicate power. Here are some suggestions from résumé expert Tim Haft (1997): *management skills:* directed, formed, governed, instituted, managed, produced; *organizational skills:* coordinated, implemented, installed, planned, prepared; *communication skills:* conducted, demonstrated, explained, instructed, lectured, reported; *research skills*: analyzed, audited, documented, evaluated, researched, tested; *creativity:* authored, conceived, created, designed, devised, originated.

> *A résumé is a balance sheet without any liabilities.*
>
> —ROBERT HALF

INTERVIEWING EXERCISE

Preparing Your Résumé

Use a résumé in this book as a model—or select one from one of the many websites—to prepare your own résumé. When it is completed try to get some feedback from your instructor, from counselors at your college's career center, from more experienced interviewees, and, if at all possible, from a professional interviewer.

The Résumé Cover Letter Along with your résumé, send a cover letter and give it the same care and attention to detail that you used in creating your résumé. Here are a few suggestions:

- Follow standard format for setting up your letter. If you're unfamiliar with the format for business letters, let the word processing wizard help you out or follow the format in the template presented in Figure 11 on page 48.

- Personalize your letter. Don't create one generic letter for all your applications; personalize each one for the specific job.

- Be sure to provide up-to-date and totally accurate contact information. At the same time, avoid including personal information in your letter or in your résumé. For example, your age, religion, and social security number should **not** be included.

- Don't duplicate the information in your résumé but do express your interest in the job and your belief that you have the competences to contribute to the company.

- Keep your letter to one page; if it's too long, it might not get read.

- Express appreciation for being considered for the position and that you look forward to hearing back.

Prepare Answers and Questions

If the interview is at all important to you, you'll probably think about it for some time. Use this time productively by rehearsing (by yourself or, if possible, with friends) the predicted course of the interview.

▼ ONLINE HELP

In addition to the Berkeley website from which the cover letter sample was taken, visit the excellent website for cover letters provided by St. Cloud State University (http://leo.stcloudstate.edu/resumes/coverlet/). Included here is useful information on how to write cover letters and a variety of sample cover letters. Also see Western Michigan's career website for more on cover letters (http://homepages.wmich.edu/ ~k7gunder/resumecover.htm).

⟶ Your street address
City, State Zip Code
Email address
(Area Code) Phone Number
Month Date, Year

Mr./Ms./Dr. First and Last Name of Person
Position or Title
Employer Organization's Name
Employer Street Address/P.O. Box
City, State Zip Code

Dear Mr./Ms./Dr. Last Name of Addressee:

Tell the reader why you are writing (i.e., regarding the position in which you are interested; if appropriate, indicate how you learned of the position and/or organization). State when you will be available.

Explain why you have targeted this particular organization: in so doing, demonstrate your knowledge of its products, services and operations. (This means you must research the potential employer.) Stress what you have *to offer*, not what you want *from*, the employer. Identify those parts of your experience (paid or non-paid) which will be of interest to this employer. Students and recent graduates should draw attention to relevant course work, special projects and campus activities. In some cases, you will add detail to items included in your resume. Refer the reader to your enclosed résumé for additional information.

Demonstrate your understanding of the duties of the position in which you are interested, and state how your unique qualifications fit the position.

Request an interview appointment, or tell the reader that you will contact him/her soon in order to see if you can schedule a mutually convenient appointment. If the employer is some distance away, indicate when you would be available for an interview. (For example, if you will be traveling to the employer's location during an academic holiday, indicate the days you will be in that area.) Thank the reader for his/her time and consideration.

Sincerely,

**This information may also
be set at left margin** ⟶ *Sign your name here*

Type your name

Enclosure

Figure 11
A Sample Résumé Cover Letter Template
From Berkeley Career Center http://career.berkeley.edu/Guidepix/letters.pdf.

Think about the questions that are likely to be asked and how you'll answer them. Table 1 presents a list of questions commonly asked in employment interviews organized around the major topics on the résumé and drawn from a vari-

? WHAT DO YOU SAY?
You know the job interviewer is going to ask about the large gap in your employment history when you roamed through Europe for two years just "to smell the roses." *What do you say?*

ety of interviewing experts (Seidman, 1991; Kennedy, 2000; Stewart & Cash, 2002). As you read this list, visualize yourself at a job interview and try responding to the questions in the middle column. After you've formulated a specific response, look at the suggestions opposite each set of questions. Did you follow the suggestions? Can you rephrase your responses for greater effectiveness? You may also find it helpful to rehearse with this list before going into the interview. Although not all of these questions will be asked in any one interview, be prepared to answer all of them. Realize that many interviewers will base much of their impression of you on the basis of your previous performance, which they take as an indication of your future performance. Keep this in mind when you discuss your previous positions and work patterns.

Even though the interviewer will ask most of the questions, you too will want to ask questions. In addition to rehearsing some answers to predicted questions, fix firmly in mind the questions you want to ask the interviewer. If this were an interview for a college teaching position, you might ask about the opportunities to develop new courses or for team teaching, the facilities for computerizing instruction, or the interests of the students at the college.

After the preparations, you're ready for the actual interview. Several suggestions may guide you through this sometimes difficult procedure.

Make an Effective Presentation of Self

This is probably the most important part of the entire procedure. If you fail here and make a bad initial impression, it will be difficult to

TABLE 1   **Common Interview Questions**

As you read through this table, consider how you'd answer these common questions.

Question Areas	Examples	Suggestions
Objectives and Career Goals	What made you apply to Datacomm? Do you know much about Datacomm? What do you like most about Datacomm? If you took a job with us, where would you like to be in five years? What benefits do you want to get out of this job?	Be positive (and as specificas you can be) about the company. Demonstrate your company. Take a long-range view; no firm wants to hiresomeone who will be looking for another job insix months.
Education	What do you think of the education you got at Queens College? Why did you major in communication? What was majoring in communication at Queens like? What kinds of courses did you take? Did you do an internship? What were your responsibilities? Were computer skills integrated into the courses?	Be positive about your educational experience. Try to relate your educational experience to the specific job. Demonstrate competence but at the same time the willingness to continueyour education (eitherformally or informally).
Previous Work Experience	Tell me about your previous work experience. What did you do exactly? Did you enjoy working at Happy Publications? Why did you leave? How does this previous experience relate to the work you'd be doing here at Datacomm? What kinds of problems did you encounter at your last position?	Again, be positive; never knock a previous job or employer. If you do, the interviewer will think you may be criticizing them in the near future. Especially avoid specific people with whom you worked.

Question Areas	Examples	Suggestions
Special Competences	I see here you have a speaking and writing knowledge of Spanish. Could you talk with someone on the phone in Spanish or write letters in Spanish to our customers? Do you know any other languages? How much do you know about computers? Do you know Excel? PowerPoint? Accessing databases? Could you prepare company bro-chures and newsletters?	Before going into the interview, review your competences. Explain your skills in as much detail as needed to establish their relevance to the job and your own specific competences.
Personal	Tell me who you are. What do you like? What do you dislike? Are you willing to relocate? Are there places you would not consider relocating to? Do you think you'd have any trouble giving orders to others? Do you have difficulty working under deadlines?	Place yourself in the position of the interviewer and ask yourself what kind of person you would hire. Stress your ability to work independently but also as a member of a team. Stress your flexibility in adapting to new work situations.
References	Do the people you listed here know you personally or academically? Which of these people know you the best? Who would give you the best reference? Who else might know about your abilities that we might contact that isn't listed here?	Be sure the people you list know you well and especially that they have special knowledge about you that is relevant to the job at hand.

Job applicants do not always act in their own best interests.

—ROBERT HALF

salvage the rest of the interview, so devote special care to the way you present yourself. Bring with you the appropriate materials, whatever they may be. At the very least bring a pen and paper, an extra copy or two of your résumé, and, if appropriate, a business card. If you're applying for a job in an area in which you've worked before, you might bring samples of your previous work. If you have the opportunity, ask what materials you should bring.

An interesting perspective on self-presentation is provided by the theory of self-monitoring, which argues that you regulate (often automatically and without any conscious thought) the way you present yourself to best achieve the effect you want (Snyder, 1987). So if you think the interviewer favors an outspoken and direct style, you'll present yourself as outspoken and direct. Self-monitoring, as you can appreciate, is especially prevalent in the employment interview, where so much depends on your making the right impression.

If you're interviewing at even a reasonably successful organization, then you're likely to be facing an interviewer who is sophisticated and who will be able to pick up on your subtle cues that may indicate annoyance, lack of confidence, lack of adequate preparation, or any other feeling that might be evaluated negatively. If you're a beginning job seeker, you're not likely to fool a seasoned interviewer. And this realization should actually provide a comforting thought: Because the interviewer, we assume, is going to see the real you, you might as well be yourself (but yourself at your best). In "being yourself" you'll feel more comfortable and are likely to communicate more effectively and present yourself with greater confidence.

When they ask about hobbies, you must tell them the only hobbies you enjoy are active ones. . . . You participate in sports, particularly status sports such as golf or tennis. You're not an observer, you're an active participant.

—JOHN T. MOLLOY

Dress for Interview Success

Many jobs are won or lost on the basis of physical appearance alone, so also give attention to your physical presentation. Unfortunately, there is no universally appropriate attire for an interview. It depends on a number of factors, perhaps first of which is the job itself. Generally, low-level jobs (cashiers in fast-food restaurants for example) have fewer dress requirements than higher-level jobs. In fact, the higher you go up the hierarchy, the more formal, more conservative, and more expensive your clothing should be. Even this seemingly simple advice has to be qualified; some high-level tech companies are probably more relaxed about clothing than are firms offering lower-level jobs in traditionally conservative fields such as law.

Nevertheless, here are a few general dress suggestions. First, discover what the accepted and appropriate attire for the company is by visiting the company and taking careful note of the way the people dress. Then dress one or two levels more conservatively. The interviewer is likely to expect this.

Second, avoid excess in just about anything you can think of. Too much jewelry, cologne, or any one particular color is likely to call attention to your manner of dress instead of to who you are and what your competencies are.

Third, dress comfortably but not too casually. Comfortable clothing will make you feel more at ease and will help you to be yourself. If you're in doubt as to how casually you should dress, err on the side of formality; wear the tie, high heels, or dress.

Fourth, consider any outward display of body piercings and facial and hand tattoos. Although people wearing such body jewelry, for example, may wish to communicate positive meanings, those interpreting these messages seem to infer that the wearer is communicating an unwillingness to conform to social norms and a willingness to take greater risks than those without such adornments (Forbes, 2001)—qualities that may work against your "fitting in." It's also worth noting that in a study of employers' perceptions, applicants with eyebrow piercings were rated and ranked significantly lower than those without such piercings (Acor, 2001).

Tattoos—temporary or permanent—may be popular at the clubs but may work against you in a job interview. Tattooed students see themselves as more adventurous, creative, individualistic, and risk-taking than those without tattoos (Drews, Allison, & Probst, 2000). Whether employers will also see the same qualities, however, is another issue.

> *If you want to succeed, you'd better look as if you mean business.*
>
> —JEANNE HOLM

Arrive on Time

In interview situations "on time" means 5 to 10 minutes early. This brief period will allow you time to relax, to get accustomed to the general surroundings, and perhaps to fill out any forms that may be required. And it gives you a cushion should something delay you on the way.

Be sure you know the name of the company, the job title, and the interviewer's name. Although you'll have much on your mind when you go into the interview, the interviewer's name is not one of the things you can afford to forget (or mispronounce).

In presenting yourself, don't err on the side of too much casualness or too much formality. When there's doubt, act on the side of increased formality. Slouching back in the chair, smoking, and chewing gum or candy are obvious behaviors to avoid when you're trying to impress an interviewer.

Demonstrate Effective Interpersonal Communication

Throughout the interview, be certain that you demonstrate confidence and the effective use of the skills of interpersonal communication. Make the interviewer see you as someone who can get the job done, who is confident. At the same time, the interview is the ideal place to put into practice all the communication skills you can muster. Here, for example, are six characteristics for communicating confidence during an interview.

- *Openness.* Answer all questions asked fully and directly. Avoid one-word answers that may signal a lack of interest or knowledge. Avoid appearing to be hiding something. Take an active role in the interview. Initiate topics or questions when appropriate. Avoid appearing as a passive participant, waiting for a stimulus.

- *Positiveness.* Emphasize your positive qualities. Express positive interest in the position. Avoid statements that are critical of yourself and others. Demonstrate positiveness and respect for the interview process, the interviewer, and the company. And express positiveness for your previous employment experiences. Never bad-mouth your former employers. If you do you may be seen as a negative person or as one who will later bad-mouth the company at which you're now applying for a job.

- *Immediacy.* Connect yourself with the interviewer throughout the interview, for example, by using the interviewer's name, focusing clearly on the interviewer's remarks, and expressing responsibility for your thoughts and feelings. Maintain eye contact with the interviewer. People who avoid eye contact are often judged to be ill at ease, as though they're afraid to engage in meaningful interaction.

- *Interaction Management.* Ensure the interviewer's satisfaction by being positive, complimentary, and generally cooperative. And be brief but not overly brief. If you make a mistake, admit it. Attempting to cover up obvious mistakes communicates a lack of confidence. Only a confident person can openly admit her or his mistakes and not worry about what others will think.

- *Expressiveness.* Let your nonverbal behaviors (especially facial expression) and vocal variety reflect your verbal messages and your general enthusiasm and high energy (but not too high). Avoid fidgeting and excessive moving about. Vary your vocal rate, pitch, and pausing, for example, to best reflect your meanings (DeGroot & Motowidlo, 1999). Avoid excessive movements, especially self-touching movements. Tapping a pencil on a desk, crossing and uncrossing your legs in rapid succession, and touching your face or hair all communicate an uneasiness, a lack of social confidence. Avoid vocalized pauses—the *ers* and *ahs*—that frequently punctuate conversations and that communicate a lack of certainty and hesitation, an uncertainty about what to say. Similarly, avoid peppering your speech with "like, you know" or "I mean" interjections.

- *Other-Orientation.* Focus on the interviewer and on the company. Express agreement and ask for clarification as appropriate. But don't ask for agreement from the interviewer by using tag questions, for example, "That was appropriate, don't you think?" or by saying normally declarative sentences with a rising intonation and thereby turning them into questions, for example, "I'll arrive at nine?" Asking for agreement communicates a lack of confidence in making decisions and in expressing opinions. See the questions from the asker's point of view. Focus your eye contact and orient your body toward the interviewer. Lean forward as appropriate.

WHAT DO YOU SAY?

The job interviewer belittles your experience, which you thought was your strong point. Several times during the interview comments were made that your experiences were "in school" or "with only a few people" or some such phrase. You think your experience has more than prepared you for this job and you want to make sure the interviewer knows this. *What do you say?*

In addition to demonstrating these qualities of effectiveness, avoid behaviors that create negative impressions during employment interviews. Here are a few of the most common mistakes that others have made:

- Being unprepared; they forgot to bring their résumé, didn't show that they knew anything about the company

- Demonstrating poor communication skills; they avoided looking at the interviewer, slouched, slurred their words, spoke in an overly low or too-rapid voice, gave one-word answers, fidgeted, dressed inappropriately

- Appearing to have an unpleasant personality; they appeared defensive, cocky, lacking in assertiveness, extremely introverted, overly aggressive

- Showing little initiative; they failed to pick up on ramifications of the interviewer's questions, gave one-word answers, didn't ask questions when appropriate

- Listening ineffectively; they were easily distracted, needed to have questions repeated, failed to maintain appropriate eye contact

Acknowledge Cultural Rules and Customs

Each culture—and each organization is much like a culture—has its own rules for communicating (Barna, 1991; Ruben, 1985; Spitzberg, 1991; Spitzberg & Cupach, 2002). These rules—whether in the interview situation or in friendly conversation—prescribe appropriate and inappropriate behavior, rewards and punishments, and what will help you get the job and what won't. For example, general advice was given earlier to emphasize your positive qualities, to highlight your abilities, and to minimize any negative characteristics or failings. But in some cultures—

especially collectivist cultures such as China, Korea, and Japan—interviewees are expected to show modesty (Copeland & Griggs, 1985). Should you stress your own competences too much, you may be seen as arrogant, brash, and unfit to work in an organization in which teamwork and cooperation are valued and expected.

In collectivist cultures great deference is to be shown to the interviewer, who represents the company. If you don't treat the interviewer with great respect, you may appear to be disrespectful of the entire company. On the other hand, in an individualist culture such as the United States, too much deference may make you appear unassertive, unsure of yourself, and unable to assume a position of authority.

And recall (as mentioned earlier) that cultures also vary greatly in attitudes toward directness. Too direct an approach may offend people of one culture, whereas too indirect an approach might offend people of another.

INTERVIEW FOR ANALYSIS

Displaying Communication Confidence in the Employment Interview

Presented below is a brief dialogue that might take place during an initial interview for a job. Read through the transcript and identify the elements that demonstrate the possession of or the lack of confidence and indicate how the applicant might have better represented herself as a more confident, a more in-control type of individual. How you would have demonstrated confidence in responding to each of Ms. Bass's questions? *What specific signals are the most important in communicating confidence in an interview?*

(continued)

Ms. Bass: And you are?

Linda: Sir? I mean Mrs., madam. Me? Er, I mean, yeah. Yeah, I'm Linda. Miss Giddeon. Linda Giddeon.

Ms. Bass: So, Ms. Giddeon, what can I do for you?

Linda: I'm here for, I mean I'm applying for that job, right?

Ms. Bass: So, you'd like a job with Datacomm. Is that right?

Linda: Well, er, yes. I guess so. I think I'd like that.

Ms. Bass: Tell me what you know about computers.

Linda: Well, I didn't take that many courses. But, I took some. Some good ones. Some were too time-consuming, so I didn't take them.

Ms. Bass: Well, tell me what you did take.

Linda: Well, I guess, I mean I took the regular courses. Here's my transcript.

Ms. Bass: I can read your transcript. But, I want to hear from you, exactly what you know about computers.

Linda: Well, I took courses in different aspects of computers. Programming I and II. And I took desktop publishing. Courses like that.

Ms. Bass: Instead of telling me your courses, tell me what you know.

Linda: Excuse me. I guess I'm a little nervous. I'm not very good at interviewing. In fact, this is my first interview and I really don't know what to say.

Ms. Bass: (Smiling) Are you sure you were a computer major?

Linda: Yes.

Ms. Bass: Okay, I know. Let me put it this way: do you think you can do anything for Datacomm?

Linda: Oh. Yes. I mean, I may be wrong about this but I'm pretty sure, I could do a lot, really a lot for Datacomm.

Ms. Bass: OK, Ms. Giddeon, now exactly what can you do for Datacomm that the next applicant can't do better?

Linda: Oh, well, I really don't know much about Datacomm. I mean, I may be wrong about this, but I thought I would assist someone and learn the job that way.

Ms. Bass: Right. What skills can you bring to Datacomm? Why would you make such a good learner?

Linda: Gee, this isn't as easy as I thought it would be.

Ms. Bass: Ms. Giddeon, tell me what you are especially good at.

Linda: Well, I guess I'm kind of good at getting along with people—you know, working with people in groups.

Ms. Bass: No, I'm not sure I know what that means. Tell me.

Linda: Like, I mean I'm pretty good at just working with people. People think I'm kind of neat. You know like people like me. I don't know, I guess it's just my personality.

Ms. Bass: I don't doubt that, Ms. Giddeon, but do you have any other talents—other than being "neat"?

Linda: I can run a desktop publishing program. Is that important?

Ms. Bass: Ms. Giddeon, everything is important.

Linda: Is there anything else?

Ms. Bass: I don't know, Ms. Giddeon, is there anything else?

Linda: I don't know.

Ms. Bass: I want to thank you for your time, Ms. Giddeon. We'll be in touch with you.

Linda: Oh, I got the job?

Ms. Bass: Not exactly. If we decide on you, we will call you.

Linda: OK.

Mentally Review the Interview

By reviewing the interview, you'll fix it firmly in your mind. What questions were asked? How did you answer them? Review and write down any important information the interviewer gave. Ask yourself what you could have done more effectively. Consider what you did effectively that you could repeat in other interviews. Ask yourself how you might correct your weaknesses and capitalize on your strengths.

Follow Up

Follow up an interview with a letter. All such letters should include an expression of thanks for the interview. In addition, however, the letter can serve any number of additional purposes. Among the most important of these are:

- to recall the interview, to stress your continued interest in the position, and to reiterate one or two of your greatest assets for this job.

- to add information not covered in the interview or that happened after the interview.

- to inquire about the position if you haven't received a response by a preset or some reasonable amount of time.

- to keep the door open after rejection for the possibility of a similar opening in the near future.

Figures 12, 13, and 14 provide examples of follow-up letters that include these functions; the marginal notes identify, more specifically, the several goals.

Rita Williams
123 Main Street
Accord, New York 12404
(845) 555-1234
Rita.Williams@nomail.com

Ms. Claire Trevor
ABC Books
321 Elm Street
Kingston, New York 12426

December 1, 2008

Dear Ms. Trevor:

1 Thank you for interviewing me on November 30, 2008 for the position of editorial assistant. As I mentioned at the interview I'm very interested in the position; it's exactly what I'm looking for.

2 As we discussed during the interview I've had an extensive background in English and communication – the areas you noted as crucial to the position. And, although we didn't have time to discuss it, I'm also most competent in all the Microsoft Office programs for both PCs and Macs.

3 I also want to add that just yesterday I was appointed editor of the college newspaper, a position I'll hold until graduation in June. It's going to be an exciting adventure; I'm looking forward to the challenge.

4 Again, thank you for your consideration. I look forward to hearing from you.

Sincerely,

Rita Williams

Rita Williams

Figure 12
A Sample Follow-Up Letter to Reiterate Interest and Competencies and to Add New Information

① This paragraph thanks the interviewer, recalls the interview, and reiterates your interest in the position. Avoid going into too much detail; the letter should not be longer than one page.

② Here you restate your major assests or competencies and even add one that wasn't discusssed at the interview. Avoid overdoing this. Your résumé and your interview should have accomplished this general goal of establishing your competencies. Use this letter as a brief reminder.

③ This adds new information and, in this case, demonstrates your confidence, willingness to take on major responsibilities, and a recognition by others of your competence to handle such a position.

④ A simple closing of thanks and continued interest will serve well here.

Rita Williams
123 Main Street
Accord, New York 12404
(845) 555-1234
Rita.Williams@nomail.com

Ms. Claire Trevor
ABC Books
321 Elm Street
Kingston, New York 12426

December 1, 2008

Dear Ms. Trevor:

❶ I'm very sorry to hear that I was not selected for the position of editorial assistant for which I interviewed on November 30, 2008.

❷ I'm still very interested in working at ABC Books and hope that you'll consider me for any similar positions that may open in the near future.

❸ I'm continuing my preparation to enter publishing by taking Advanced Editing and Print Media this semester and a course in Publishing Economics at the Learning Annex.

❹ If you have a moment, I'd much appreciate any feedback you might want to give me to help me in future interviews. I'm especially concerned with learning how I can strengthen both my résumé and my interviewing for similar positions.

❺ Thank you for your time and consideration.

Sincerely,

Rita Williams

Rita Williams

Figure 13
A Sample Follow-Up Letter to Keep the Doors Open After Rejection

❶ Here you recall the interview and state your disappointment in not being hired. Avoid blaming ("I didn't feel well that day" or "I was nervous") or guessing why you didn't get the job ("I guess my grades weren't that good").

❷ Here you reiterate your interest in the company and ask that you continue to be considered for another, similar position. Any more than this would be too much.

❸ Here you add to your list of assests that may make your résumé look better than it did originally. It demonstrates your commitment to the field and your focus on improving your knowledge and skills.

❹ If you're beginning your employment interviewing, it's often helpful to get professional feedback on your résumé as well as on your interviewing technique. Many interviewers will be reluctant to be as honest as you'd like them to be but some may say something you'll find useful in subsequent interviews. At times, this request for feedback is communicated in a separate letter. This paragraph provides an example of what you might say.

❺ A simple expression of appreciation will work best as a closing.

Rita Williams
123 Main Street
Accord, New York 12404
(845) 555-1234
Rita.Williams@nomail.com

Ms. Claire Trevor
ABC Books
321 Elm Street
Kingston, New York 12426

December 1, 2008

Dear Ms. Trevor:

1 I interviewed for the position of editorial assistant on November 30, 2008, and I'm wondering if you've made a decision. My résumé and other application materials are on file at your office. If there is any additional information I can supply please let me know.

2 I am very interested in working at ABC Books and feel that my academic courses, my work on the student newspaper, and my lifelong love of books would make me a great editorial assistant.

3 Thank you for your time and consideration. I look forward to hearing from you.

Sincerely,

Rita Williams

Rita Williams

Figure 14
Sample Follow-Up Letter to Inquire Whether a Decision Has Been Made

1 At times, it may be necessary to inquire if a decision has been made. For example, if this job is your first choice but if your second choice made you an offer, then it's important to make inquiry. Always do this courteously (even if your natural inclination is to be annoyed at the delay); there may be quite reasonable explanations for the delay. Asking if you can send any additional information you can helps to stress your continued interest in the position.

2 Here you reiterate your interest in the company and your major assets – briefly but clearly.

3 A simple thank you and a reasonable request to hear some kind of response.

Writing the Follow-Up Letter

Select one of the following situations and write a brief follow-up letter. Use fictional names for yourself and the interviewer.

- Letter to thank the interviewee for the information interview
- Letter to thank the interviewer for the job interview
- Letter to request information because you haven't had any response about the job
- Letter to express regret at not getting the job

You may find it helpful to form groups of five or six and discuss these letters in terms of their effectiveness to achieve your purpose. You may also want to get some feedback from experts in the field.

The Lawfulness of Questions

Through the Equal Employment Opportunity Commission, the federal government has classified some interview questions as unlawful. These are federal guidelines and therefore apply in all 50 states; individual states, however, may have additional restrictions. You may find it interesting to take the following self-test (constructed with the good help of Stewart & Cash, 2002; Zincoff & Goyer, 1984; Kirby, 2001) to see if you can identify which questions are lawful and which are unlawful (see Pullum, 1991).

> *'Tis not every question that deserves an answer.*
> —THOMAS FULLER

Test Yourself

CAN YOU IDENTIFY UNLAWFUL QUESTIONS?

For each question write L (lawful) if you think the question is legal for an interviewer to ask in an employment interview and U (unlawful) if you think the question is illegal. For each question you consider unlawful, indicate why you think it's so classified.

_____ ❶ Are you married, Tom?

_____ ❷ When did you graduate from high school, Mary?

_____ ❸ Do you have a picture so I can attach it to your résumé?

_____ ❹ Will you need to be near a mosque (church, synagogue)?

_____ ❺ I see you taught courses in "gay and lesbian studies." Are you gay?

_____ ❻ Is Chinese your native language?

_____ ❼ Will you have difficulty getting a babysitter?

_____ ❽ I notice that you walk with a limp. Is this a permanent injury?

_____ ❾ Where were you born?

_____ ❿ Have you ever been arrested for a crime?

_____ ⓫ How tall are you? How much do you weigh?

_____ ⓬ I see you were in the Army. Were you honorably discharged?

All twelve questions are unlawful. The remaining discussion illustrates why each of these and similar questions are unlawful.

Recognizing Unlawful Questions Some of the more important areas in which unlawful questions are frequently asked concern age, marital status, race, religion, nationality, citizenship, physical condition, and arrest and criminal records. For example, it's legal to ask applicants whether they meet the legal age requirements for the job and could provide proof of that. But it's unlawful to ask their exact age, even in indirect ways as illustrated in question 2 in the self-test. It's unlawful to ask about a person's marital status (question 1) or about family matters that are unrelated to the job (question 7). An interviewer may ask you, however, to identify a close relative or guardian if you're a minor or any relative who currently works for the company.

Questions concerning your race (questions 3 and 6), religion (question 4), national origin (question 9), affectional orientation (question 5), age (question 2), handicaps unrelated to job performance (question 8), or even arrest record (question 10) are unlawful, as are questions that get at this same information in oblique ways. For example, requiring a picture may be a way of discriminating against an applicant on the basis of sex, race, or age.

Thus, for example, the interviewer may ask you in what languages you're fluent but may not ask what your native language is (question 6), what language you speak at home, or what language your parents speak. The interviewer may ask you if you are in this country legally but may not ask if you were born in this country or naturalized (question 9). The interviewer may ask about the type of training you received in the military but not if you were honorably discharged (question 12).

The interviewer may inquire into your physical condition only insofar as the job is concerned. For example, the interviewer may ask, "Do you have any physical problems that might prevent you from fulfilling the responsibilities of this job?" But the interviewer may not ask about any physical disabilities (question 8) or about your height or weight (question 11). The interviewer may ask you if you've been convicted of a felony but not if you've been arrested (question 10).

▼ ONLINE HELP

If you have questions about disability disclosure and interviewing, take a look at Jan's Consultants' Corner (www.jan.wvu.edu/corner/vol01/iss13.htm).

These are merely examples of some of the lawful and unlawful questions that may be asked during an interview. Note that even the questions used as examples here might be lawful in specific situations. The test to apply is simple: Is the information related to your ability to perform the job? Such questions are referred to as BFOQ—bona fide occupational qualification—questions.

Once you've discovered what kinds of questions are unlawful, consider how to deal with them if they come up during an interview.

Dealing with Unlawful Questions   There are three main approaches to dealing with unlawful questions. In selecting your approach, realize that answering or not answering a question—whether it is legal or illegal—may well make the difference between getting the job and not getting the job. Keep this in mind as you select your strategy. Also, note that at times an interviewer may ask a question that is technically illegal but may not even know it's illegal. Or the interviewer may have no discriminatory or negative motives for asking it.

> *The things most people want to know are usually none of their business.*
> —GEORGE BERNARD SHAW

Answer the Question.   The most obvious strategy is to simply answer the question, assuming you have no reason to suspect any negative motives on the part of the interviewer and you don't mind answering this question, even though you know it's illegal. And do realize that even when a question is technically illegal, your not answering it may work against your getting the job. The interviewer may see you as unnecessarily argumentative and not a cooperative future member of the team.

Answer the Question (In Part).   Another strategy is to answer the part of the question you don't object to and omit any information you don't want to give. For example, if you're asked an unlawful question concerning what language is spoken at home, you may respond with a statement such as "I have some language facility in German and Italian," without specifying a direct answer to the question. If you're asked to list all the organizations of which you're a member (an unlawful question in many states, because it's often a way of getting at political affiliation, religion, nationality, and various other areas), you might respond by saying something like: "The only organizations I belong to that are relevant to this job are the International Communication Association and the National Communication Association."

This type of response is preferable to the one that immediately tells the interviewer she or he is asking an unlawful question, which can easily create an adversarial relationship where you are pitted against the interviewer. As already noted, it's possible that the interviewer isn't even aware of the legality of various questions and may have no intention of trying to get at information you're not obliged to give. For example, the interviewer may recognize the nationality of your last name and simply want to mention that she or he is also of that nationality. If you immediately take issue with the question, you may be creating problems where none really exist.

On the other hand, recognize that in many employment interviews the unwritten intention is to keep certain people out, whether it's people who are older or those of a particular marital status, affectional orientation, nationality, religion, and so on. If you're confronted by questions that are unlawful and that you don't want to answer, and if the gentle methods described above don't work and your interviewer persists—saying, for example, "Is German the language spoken at home?" or "What other organizations have you belonged to?"—you might counter by saying that such information is irrelevant to the interview and to the position you're seeking. Again, be courte-

---

▼ ONLINE HELP

The career services department of Minot State University maintains a useful website on interviewing techniques and sample questions. Take a look (www.minotstateu.edu/careers/interviewingtechniques.html).

ous but firm. Say something like, "This position does not call for any particular language skill and so it does not matter what language is spoken in my home." Or you might say, "The organizations I mentioned are the only relevant ones; whatever other organizations I belong to will certainly not interfere with my ability to perform in this company at this job."

Explain Your Reasons for Not Answering. If the interviewer still persists—and it's doubtful that many would after these rather clear and direct responses—you might note that these questions are unlawful and that you'd rather not answer them. This response at least gives you a convenient way out of the situation just in case the interviewer didn't realize that these questions are, in fact, illegal. Again, if the interviewer persists and you don't want to answer the questions, say so.

INTERVIEWING EXERCISE

Responding to Unlawful Questions

This exercise is designed to raise some of the unlawful questions that you don't have to answer and provide you with practice in developing responses that protect your privacy while maintaining a positive relationship with the interviewer. In the self-test, Can You Identify Unlawful Questions? 12 questions were presented. Assuming that you do not want to answer the questions, how would you respond to each of them? One useful procedure is to write your responses and then compare them with those of other students, either in groups or with the class as a whole. Or form two-person groups and role-play the interviewer–interviewee situation. To make this exercise realistic, the person playing the interviewer should press for an answer, while the interviewee should continue to avoid answering, yet respond positively and cordially. You'll discover this is not always easy; tempers often flare in this type of interaction.

EMPLOYMENT INTERVIEW PREPARATION GUIDE

Before entering the employment interview, prepare yourself by completing the following questionnaire. It will not be easy; in fact, it's likely to prove frustrating and quite difficult. But it will be helpful. This preparation will make you more informed and more focused, help you anticipate and practice likely interview questions and answers, and put you more at ease and in control of the interview process.

1. **Information about self.** What do you want the interviewer to know and notice about you? In the left column list four things about yourself that are not on your résumé that you want to highlight, and in the right column indicate how you'll communicate these things to the interviewer.

Things about Myself That I Want the Interviewer to Know	How I'll Communicate These Things to the Interviewer
1.	1.
2.	2.
3.	3.
4.	4.

2. **Knowledge of company.** Will you be able to demonstrate your knowledge of the company (for example, its primary and secondary businesses, its immediate and long-term objectives, its competition)? Write a paragraph demonstrating your knowledge about the company that includes at least three facts about the company that might prove relevant during the interview.

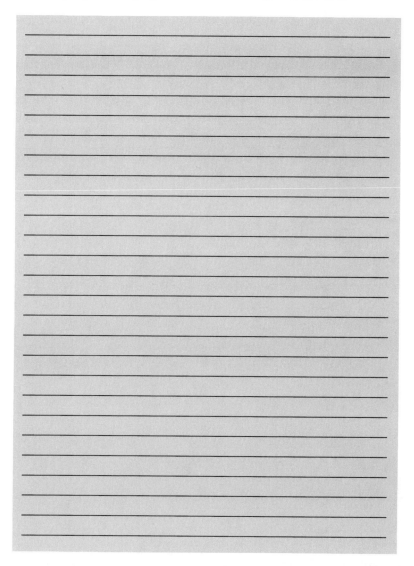

3. **Knowledge of position.** Will you be able to demonstrate your knowledge of the position for which you're applying (the qualifications, the responsibilities, how this job fits in with the entire organization, salary range)? Write a paragraph that includes at least three facts about the position that might prove relevant during the interview.

4. **Special skills.** What special skills or competences might you be asked about (for example, what presentation skills do you have?) and how might you demonstrate your competences (for example, you took a class in public speaking and used Power-Point throughout the course)?

Special Skills I Might Be Asked About	How I'll Demonstrate These Skills
1. _____	1. _____
2. _____	2. _____
3. _____	3. _____
4. _____	4. _____

5. **Information to learn.** What do you want to learn from the interviewer? List four things you want to find out about during the interview (about the job, about the company, about your potential role in the company, about salary, etc.) and how you might discover these during the interview.

Possible Questions I May Be Asked	Possible Answers I Could Give
1. _____	1. _____
_____	_____
_____	_____
_____	_____
_____	_____
_____	_____
2. _____	2. _____
_____	_____
_____	_____
_____	_____
_____	_____
3. _____	3. _____
_____	_____
_____	_____
_____	_____
_____	_____
4. _____	4. _____
_____	_____
_____	_____
_____	_____
_____	_____

6. **Contributions.** What can you contribute to the company? List four things you can do for the company that you may want to bring out during the interview. Next to each one, indicate what you can say to demonstrate your ability to make these contributions.

Information I Want to Know	How I'll Discover This Information
1. _____	1. _____
2. _____	2. _____
3. _____	3. _____
4. _____	4. _____

7. **Likely questions.** What are you likely to be asked? List four questions that you'll possibly be asked and what you believe to be effective answers. If you anticipate problems (for example, on the basis of experience, education, age, or any number of other issues) include the questions that might raise these issues along with your anticipated answers.

Contributions I Can Make	Evidence That I Can Make Such Contributions
1. _____	1. _____
_____	_____
_____	_____
_____	_____
_____	_____
_____	_____
2. _____	2. _____
_____	_____
_____	_____
_____	_____
_____	_____
3. _____	3. _____
_____	_____
_____	_____
_____	_____
_____	_____
4. _____	4. _____
_____	_____
_____	_____
_____	_____
_____	_____

8. **Unlawful questions.** What unlawful questions might you be asked? List three unlawful questions you may be asked and the way in which you could answer them.

Possible Unlawful Questions I May Be Asked	Possible Answers I Could Give
1. _____	1. _____
2. _____	2. _____
3. _____	3. _____

Continuing Your Study of Interviewing

Interviewing is likely to be a significant part of your professional life, so it will help to renew your skills periodically or to simply keep abreast of the latest thinking about effective interviewing. There are lots of ways to do this.

When you're in a bookstore—a brick-and-mortar or an online one—take a look at the interviewing section. If something seems particularly interesting or relevant, read it.

Most web browsers frequently highlight articles on interviewing. Make it a practice to look at these occasionally. If you want a more intense dose, set a Google alert to "interviewing tips" or—if you really want lots of references—use *interviewing* without modification. When you see something that might prove interesting, take a look at it or save it to your new "interviewing" folder.

If you want more experience in interviewing, take a course (or another course) in interviewing, either in college or at your local adult education center.

Summary of Concepts and Skills

This book introduced the process of interviewing, explored the nature of questions and answers, and identified the major forms of interviewing (focusing on information gathering and employment interviews).

1. Interviewing is a form of interpersonal communication in which two persons interact largely through a question-and-answer format to achieve specific goals.

2. The interview process can, for convenience, be visualized as a series of stages: opening, feedforward, question-and-answer session, feedback, and closing.

3. Questions may be viewed as varying in their degree of bias (whether neutral or leading), openness, primacy (whether primary or follow-up), and directness.

4. In informative interviews the following guidelines should prove useful: select the person you wish to interview, secure an appointment, prepare your questions, establish rapport with the interviewee, ask permission to tape the interview, ask open-ended questions, and follow up the interview.

5. Especially important to the job interview is the résumé, which may be chronological, functional, or in the form of a curriculum vitae, and the cover letter that accompanies the résumé.

6. In employment interviews the following guidelines should prove useful: prepare yourself intellectually and physically for the interview, establish your objectives, prepare answers to predicted questions, make an effective presentation of yourself, mentally review the interview, and close and follow up the interview.

7. Job interviewees should familiarize themselves with possible unlawful questions and develop strategies for dealing with them.

Throughout, this book stressed the practical skills of interviewing. Place a check mark next to those skills you feel you need to work on.

_____ 1. I follow the basic guidelines in conducting informative interviews.

_____ 2. Before the interview I prepare myself intellectually and physically, establish my objectives as clearly as I can, and prepare answers to predicted questions.

_____ 3. During the interview I make an effective presentation of myself and demonstrate effective interpersonal communication skills.

_____ 4. After the interview I mentally review the interview and follow it up with a letter.

_____ 5. I can frame and respond appropriately to questions varying in terms of neutral–biased, openness–closedness, primary–follow-up, and direct–indirect.

_____ 6. I can recognize and respond appropriately to unlawful questions.

The **Interviewing**
Guidebook

Glossary

appraisal interview. A type of **interview** in which the interviewee's performance is assessed by management or by more experienced colleagues.

BFOQ. Bona fide occupational qualification questions, as opposed to questions that are illegal.

chronological résumé. A type of **résumé** that organizes experience and job titles beginning with the most recent or current position and working back through the work history.

confidence. A quality of interpersonal effectiveness; a comfortable, at-ease feeling in interpersonal communication situations.

counseling interview. A type of **interview** in which the interviewer tries to learn about the interviewee in an attempt to provide some form of guidance, advice, or insight.

cover letter. A letter of introduction that accompanies the job résumé.

cultural rules. Rules that are specific to a given cultural group and that members are expected to follow.

curriculum vitae. A type of **résumé** used by professors, scientists, and others that lists their accomplishments, writings, discoveries, and service.

employment interview. A type of **interview** in which the interviewee is questioned to ascertain his or her suitability for a particular job.

exit interview. A type of **interview** in which the departing employee and management discuss the reasons for the employee's leaving the organization.

follow-up letters. Letters sent after an interview to thank the interviewer or interviewee and, in the case of employment interviews, to advance the likelihood of your getting the job (or a job).

functional résumé. A type of **résumé** that organizes experience in terms of competences or skills.

group norm. Rule or expectation of appropriate behavior for a member of a group or organization.

guided interview. An interview structure in which questions are chosen in advance but are treated flexibly and in response to the ongoing interaction.

informal interview. An interview format that has little rigid structure.

information interview. A type of **interview** in which the interviewer asks the interviewee, usually a person of some reputation and accomplishment, questions designed to elicit his or her views, predictions, and perspectives on specific topics.

interview. A particular form of interpersonal communication in which two persons interact largely by question-and-answer format to achieve specific goals.

job shadowing. An increasingly common practice of following a person at work so that you can learn what his or her job entails.

journalistic interview. A type of **interview** in which an interviewer questions a person of some note for a wider audience.

leading question. See **neutral and leading questions.**

leave-taking cues. Verbal and nonverbal cues that indicate a desire to terminate a conversation.

networking. Enlisting the aid of others to help solve a problem, often related to finding a job.

neutral and leading questions. A classification of questions based on whether they provide no indication of what the interviewer expects (neutral) or do indicate what the interviewer expects or wants (leading).

open-ended and closed questions. A classification of questions based on the freedom of response allowed, ranging from total freedom (open-ended) to a simple yes or no (closed).

persuasive interview. A type of **interview** in which the interviewer attempts to change the interviewee's attitudes or behavior.

primary and follow-up questions. A classification of questions based on whether they introduce a topic (primary) or ask for some additional information on a topic already raised (follow-up).

quantitative interview. A type of interview structure in which response choices are identified in advance so that they can be measured and statistical analysis applied.

résumé. A summary of essential information about an individual's experience, education, and abilities; also see **chronological résumé, functional résumé,** and **curriculum vitae.**

standard open interview. An interview structure designed for interviewing a variety of job candidates and having prearranged and ordered questions that are asked similarly of each applicant.

survey interview. A type of **interview** in which an interviewer seeks responses from a number of people with a carefully prepared series of questions, often designed to yield statistical data.

unlawful questions. Questions that are legally prohibited in a job interview, focusing on, for example, age, arrest record, or religion.

Bibliography

Acor, A. A. (2001). Employers' perceptions of persons with body art and an experimental test regarding eyebrow piercing. PhD dissertation, Marquette University. *Dissertation Abstracts International: Second B: The Sciences and Engineering,* 61, 3885.

Ayres, J., Ayres, D. M., & Sharp, D. (1993). A progress report on the development of an instrument to measure communication apprehension in employment interviews. *Communication Research Reports* 10, 87–94.

Barna, L. M. (1991). Stumbling blocks in intercultural communication. In L. A. Samovar & R. E. Porter (Eds.), *Intercultural communication: A reader,* 4th ed. (pp. 345–352). Belmont, CA: Wadsworth.

Copeland, L., & Griggs, L. (1985). *Going international: How to make friends and deal effectively in the global marketplace.* New York: Random House.

DeGroot, T., & Motowidlo, S. J. (1999). Why visual and vocal interview cues can affect interviewers' judgments and predict job performance. *Journal of Applied Psychology,* 84 (December), 986–993.

Drews, D. R., Allison, C. K., & Probst, J. R. (2000). Behavioral and self-concept differences in tattooed and nontattooed college students. *Psychological Reports,* 86, 475–481.

Forbes, G. B. (2001). College students with tattoos and piercings: Motives, family experiences, personality factors, and perception by others. *Psychological Reports,* 89, 774–786.

Haft, T. (1997). *Résumés.* Princeton, NJ: Princeton Review.

Hambrick, R. S. (1991). *The management skills builder: Self-directed learning strategies for career development.* New York: Praeger.

Kanter, A. B. (1995). *The essential book of interviewing: Everything you need to know from both sides of the table.* New York: Random House [Times Books].

Kennedy, J. L. (2000). *Job interviews for dummies*. New York: Hungry Minds.

Kirby, D. (2001, January 30). Finessing interviews: Don't ask, do tell. *New York Times*, G2.

Powell, L., & Amsbary, J. (2006). *Interviewing: Situations and contexts*. Boston: Allyn & Bacon.

Pullum, S. J. (1991). Illegal questions in the selection interview: Going beyond contemporary business and professional communication textbooks. *Bulletin of the Association for Business Communication*, 54 (September), 36–43.

Rector, M., & Neiva, E. (1996). Communication and personal relationships in Brazil. In W. B. Gudykunst, S. Ting-Toomey, & T. Nishida (Eds.), *Communication in personal relationships across cultures* (pp. 156–173). Thousand Oaks, CA: Sage.

Ruben, B. D. (1985). Human communication and cross-cultural effectiveness. In L. A. Samovar, & R. E. Porter (eds.), *Intercultural communication: A Reader*, 4th ed. (pp. 338–346). Belmont, CA: Wadsworth.

Seidman, I. E. (1991). *Interviewing as qualitative research: A guide for researchers in education and the social sciences*. New York: Teachers College Press.

Snyder, M. (1987). *Public appearances, private realities*. New York: W. H. Freeman.

Spitzberg, B. H. (1991). Intercultural communication competence. In L. A. Samovar & R. E. Porter (Eds.), *Intercultural communication: A reader*, 6th ed. (pp. 353–365). Belmont, CA: Wadsworth.

Spitzberg, B. H., & Cupach, W. R. (2002). Interpersonal Skills. In M. L. Knapp & J. A. Daly (Eds.), *Handbook of interpersonal communication*, 3rd ed. (pp. 564–611). Thousand Oaks, CA: Sage.

Stewart, C. J., & Cash, W. B., Jr. (2002). *Interviewing: Principles and practices*, 10th ed. New York: McGraw-Hill.

Taub, M. (1997). *Interviews*. Princeton, NJ: Princeton Review.

Zincoff, M. Z., & Goyer, R. S. (1984). *Interviewing*. New York: Macmillan.

Appendix

Additional Online Help

Here are some websites you'll find useful as you prepare for your interviews. Regardless of what school you're attending, you have available the resources of hundreds of colleges and universities. Make use of these and other sites you find; they all have something to teach.

THE UNIVERSITY of TENNESSEE

| University Links ⬍ | A-Z Index / WebMail / Dept. Directory | Enter search term Select type of search ⬍ go |

Career Services

Students
Register With Us
» **Instructions**
» **Student Login**
» **Career Services Handbook**
» **No-Show Policy**
» **Code of Conduct**
Choosing Majors
» **Getting Started**
» **Counseling and Assessments**
» **Career Classes**
» **Web Resources**
Grad School
» **Information**
Job Search Preparation
» **Job Fairs**
» **Resumes & Business Correspondence**
» **Interviewing**
» **Dining & Business Etiquette**

Interviewing
- Ace Your Job Interview Handout
- Welcome to The Job Interview (PowerPoint Presentation)
- How to Interview
- Fifty Commonly Asked Interview Questions
- Self-Assessment for Interviewing
- How to Ask Questions in a Job Interview
- Questions Commonly Asked of Interviewers
- The Telephone Interview
- Guide to the Company Visit
- Behavioral Interviewing Strategies

Need additional information? Contact: Deanna Bonner · (865)974-5435· (865)974-6497 (fax)
For technical difficulties with this site, contact Career Services WebMaster: career@utk.edu
Copyright ©2003 The University of Tennessee · Knoxville Tennessee 37996

University of Tennessee Career Services Website
(http://career.utk.edu/students/skills_interview.asp)
Reprinted with permission of the University of Tennessee.

Notes

_____

_____

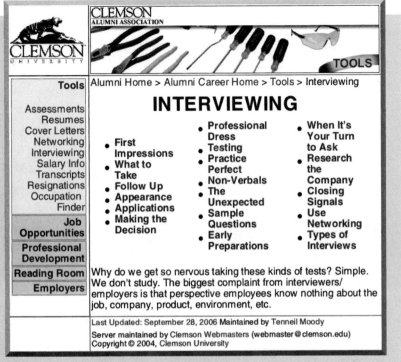

INTERVIEWING

Tools
Assessments
Resumes
Cover Letters
Networking
Interviewing
Salary Info
Transcripts
Resignations
Occupation Finder

Job Opportunities

Professional Development

Reading Room

Employers

- First Impressions
- What to Take
- Follow Up
- Appearance
- Applications
- Making the Decision

- Professional Dress
- Testing
- Practice Perfect
- Non-Verbals
- The Unexpected
- Sample Questions
- Early Preparations

- When It's Your Turn to Ask
- Research the Company
- Closing Signals
- Use Networking
- Types of Interviews

Why do we get so nervous taking these kinds of tests? Simple. We don't study. The biggest complaint from interviewers/employers is that perspective employees know nothing about the job, company, product, environment, etc.

Last Updated: September 28, 2006 Maintained by Tenneil Moody

Server maintained by Clemson Webmasters (webmaster@clemson.edu)

**Clemson University Career Services Website
(http://alumni.Clemson.edu/career/interviewing.htm)**

Notes

_____

_____

_____

_____

_____

_____

_____

_____

_____

_____

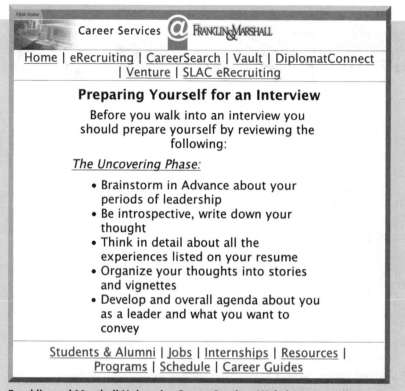

Career Services @ FRANKLIN&MARSHALL

Home | eRecruiting | CareerSearch | Vault | DiplomatConnect | Venture | SLAC eRecruiting

Preparing Yourself for an Interview

Before you walk into an interview you should prepare yourself by reviewing the following:

The Uncovering Phase:

- Brainstorm in Advance about your periods of leadership
- Be introspective, write down your thought
- Think in detail about all the experiences listed on your resume
- Organize your thoughts into stories and vignettes
- Develop and overall agenda about you as a leader and what you want to convey

Students & Alumni | Jobs | Internships | Resources | Programs | Schedule | Career Guides

Franklin and Marshall University Career Services Website (www.career.fandm.edu/interviewing/interviewprep.html)
Reprinted with permission of Franklin and Marshall University.

Notes

_____
_____
_____
_____
_____
_____
_____
_____
_____
_____

Creighton University Career Services Website
(www2.Creighton.edu/careercenter/interviewingtips/index.php)
Reprinted with permission of Creighton University.

Notes

_____

_____

_____

_____

_____

_____

_____

_____

_____

_____

_____

Index

The italicized letters *f*, *g*, and *t* following some page numbers refer to figures, glossary items, and tables respectively.

About website, 8*f*
academic vitae, 43
appointment for interview, 16
appraisal interview, 28, 87*g*

BFOQ questions, 71, 87*g*

Career Journal website, 33*f*
chronological résumé, 39, 42*f*, 87*g*
closed questions, 11, 88*g*
closing the interview, 19
closing, 7
collectivist culture, 58
confidence, 54, 58, 87*g*
continuing your study of interviewing, 82
cover letter for résumé, 46, 48*f*, 87*g*
cultural rules, 57, 87*g*
curriculum vitae, 43, 87*g*

definition of interviewing, 1
direct–indirect questions, 12
directness, 58
dressing for the interview, 53

employment interview preparation guide, 74
employment interview, 28, 87*g*
ethical considerations, 13–14
exercise
    practicing Interviewing skills, 27
    preparing your résumé, 46
    responding to unlawful questions, 73
    writing the follow-up letter, 68
exercises, 27, 46, 68, 73
exit interview, 29, 87*g*
expressiveness, 56

feedback, 6
feedforward, 6
following-up the interview, 19, 61
follow-up letters, 87g
   to express thanks, 20f
   to inquire about decision, 66f
   to keep doors open, 64f
   to reiterate interest, 62f
follow-up questions, 12, 89g
functional résumé, 39, 40f, 87g

Google website, 37f
guided interview, 7, 88g

homework, 34

immediacy, 55
Indiana University website, 30
individualist culture, 58
informal interview, 7, 88g
information interview, 14, 88g
information interview preparation guide, 21
interaction management, 55
interpersonal communication, 54
interview, 88g
interview for analysis, 58
interview questions, 9–12, 50–51t
interview structures, 7
interviewing, definition of, 1
interviewing, nature of, 1
interviews, types of
  appraisal, 28
  employment, 28
  exit, 29
  guided, 7
  information, 14
  journalistic, 3
  quantitative, 9
  standard open, 9

job shadowing, 34, 88*g*
journalistic interview, 3, 88*g*

lawfulness of questions, 68
leading questions, 10, 88*g*
leave-taking cues, 7, 88*g*
letter of thanks for informative interview, 20*f*
letters, samples of, 20, 62, 64, 66*f*
letters, types of
   follow-up to inquire about decision, 66*f*
   follow-up to keep doors open, 64*f*
   follow-up to reiterate interest, 62*f*
   thank you, 20*f*

Monster Board website, 35

networking, 29, 88*g*
neutral-leading questions, 10, 88*g*

online help, 14, 16, 28, 31, 34, 39, 43, 47, 70, 72
open-closed questions, 11, 18, 88*g*
opening, 4
openness, 11, 55
other-orientation, 56

person to interview, 15
positiveness, 55
preparation guide, for employment interview, 74
preparation guide, for informative interview, 21
primary–follow-up questions, 12, 89*g*
process of interviewing, 4

quantitative interview, 9, 89*g*
question-and-answer session, 6
questions, common interview, 50*t*
questions, types of, 9

rapport, 17
résumé, 38, 89*g*

résumé cover letter, 46
résumé cover letter template, 48*f*
résumé types, 38
résumés, samples of, 40*f*, 42
résumés, types of
   chronological, 39, 42*f*
   curriculum vitae, 43
   functional, 39, 40*f*
résumé, writing suggestions for, 45

self, presentation of, 49
stages of the interview, 5*f*
standard open interview, 9, 89*g*
survey interview, 9, 89*g*

taping the interview, 18
team interview, 3
   advantages of, 4
   disadvantages of, 4
test yourself, 68

unlawful questions, 68, 89*g*
   dealing with, 71
   recognizing, 69
   self-test of, 68

USGS website, 2*f*

websites
   About, 8*f*
   Career Journal, 33*f*
   Google, 37*f*
   Indiana University, 30*f*
   Monster Board, 35*f*
   USGS, 2
what do you say? 18, 34, 49, 56